# The Van Life
By Alexandra Van Steen

Other Titles by Alexandra Van Steen:
**-The Van Life Book: Daydream to Dream Life**
**-Secrets of a Successful Executive Assistant**

When you're finished reading this guide, please hop back over to Amazon and leave your honest review. Reviews help the guide get shared and reach more potential adventurers like yourself.

Please note, this book does contain some affiliate links. They cost you nothing extra but provide us with a small stream of income to continue life on the road. If you have any questions, please don't hesitate to reach out to us via email **fnavanlife@gmail.com** or on Instagram at **www.instagram.com/fnavanlife**. We also offer van life/van build consultation sessions at **https://fnavanlife.com/consultation/**. Thank you so much for your support, now let's hit the road.

Copyright © 2021 Alexandra Van Steen
All rights reserved.

# Contents

**Land of the Midnight Sun 5**

**Prepare for Adventure 9**

**Getting to Alaska 13**

**Cost of Travel in Alaska 19**

**The Truth About Alaskan Roads 25**

**Internet Connectivity and Cell Phone Signal 31**

**Wild Camping in Alaska 33**

**Anchorage 37**

**Seward Highway & Girdwood 45**

**Whittier 53**

**Seward 59**

**Cooper Landing 65**

**Soldotna 71**

**Homer and Seldovia 75**

**Palmer and Wasilla 81**

**Glacier View and Glennallen 89**

**Valdez 97**

**Talkeetna 105**

**Denali National Park 107**

**Fairbanks 115**

**Up North of 60 121**

**Once in a Lifetime Adventure You Have to do Again 129**

**Coordinates for Where we Slept 131**

**Accompanying YouTube Video Series 139**

**Where to Next? 141**

# Land of the Midnight Sun

The 49th state, Alaska, seems to be on every nomad's bucket list. Perhaps it's for the street credit you get for having driven thousands of miles on questionable roads, the breathtaking views around every corner, the nature and wildlife you're bound to run across or for getting so deep off-grid you're unreachable for days. Whatever the reason, within twelve hours of arriving in Anchorage, I was seriously considering moving there forever. It turns out this feeling is incredibly familiar to many of the now local Alaskans who came for a summer and never left. Every mile, every new town, every awe-inspiring mountain range, we kept thinking *this* is the most beautiful place we'd ever laid eyes on. There's no way this stunning vista could ever be topped. Then three days later, faced with an even more impressive view, you'd swear *this* was the best sight you'd ever had the privilege to witness.

Topping off all that stunning beauty, the people are so friendly and, dare I say, ballsy. It takes a certain kind of no-nonsense human being to brave an Alaskan winter – heck it's even hard living in Alaska in the summer with only a few short months of never-ending sunlight to get ready for winter.

Yet somehow, in my first few hours in this great state, I was willing to consider living with only three and a half hours of sunlight a day and endless below zero temperatures. It couldn't be that bad, could it?! It would certainly be an adventure.

Unfortunately, the answer to my Alaskan winter question will have to wait for a future version of this guidebook because as fall rolled in, we rolled out of the last frontier. Our sixty-six-day journey in Alaska was over and we were crestfallen to have to leave before we felt ready to do so. On the flip side, we were incredibly lucky to have explored Alaska for that long. Most tourist come for a long weekend, a week, maybe two at the most. They quickly realize whatever length of time they were here was not enough and start planning their next visit. Thankfully, van life affords us the luxury of time. By traveling in a van, RV, travel trailer, camper, rental car or U-Haul (more on that later), not only do you get to see and do more in Alaska, but you also save yourself thousands of dollars in transportation and hotel costs.

Alaska is not cheap, but most things worth doing rarely are. Over the years, Alaska has established herself as a tourist destination for anyone with a sense of adventure and a love of the outdoors.

We heard time and again, how its popularity has gradually driven prices up, and up, and up. Luckily, we're going to breakdown how you can save money in many places, so you can splurge on the once in a lifetime experiences your adventurous heart is craving. For example, there are endless wild and free camping sites accessible to almost any sized rig so you can save all those campground fees and turn them into an unforgettable glacier hiking expedition or jet ski ride into Blackstone Bay or bear sighting excursion during the salmon run.

This guide will lay out all of our favorite camping locations, things to do in each town, road conditions, swimming holes, hikes, excursions, grocery prices, and more. The goal is to take you along for our summer in Alaska so you can plan your best, most cost-efficient summer in Alaska too.

If you're not familiar with us here at FnA Van Life, we are so glad to meet you our fellow nomadic adventurers. Me Alex and my boyfriend Frankie had a dream to live an unconventional life. After many years in New York City, we were ready to get out of the hustle and bustle and hug a tree without the sound of sirens in the background.

On our first date, Frankie told me about his goal to live in a camper and snowboard across North America. As soon as I heard the idea, my heart jumped, and I knew it was something I needed to experience. Heck, it was already on my bucket list and here was a guy offering to make it happen in real life. Six months after that, we set a budget to save for a year so we could travel for at least twelve months and build our own camper van debt free. During our year of saving, we bought an old van and turned it into a home. On December 27th, 2019, we left New York for the unknown and haven't looked back. If you want to learn more about that process, I wrote an entire book dedicated to helping future van lifers get on the road and if you'd like to follow our many adventures since then, come find us on YouTube.

After exploring over forty states and two provinces, I can say without a doubt that Alaska has something special you won't find anywhere else. If you're reading this guide, I can only imagine that in a short time you will be seeing the awe-inspiring mountains, endless sunsets and truly wild wildlife with your own eyes I couldn't be more excited for you. My goal for this guide is to make sure you have the most amazing summer of your life, and that Alaska will deliver on all of your wildest dreams.

# Prepare for Adventure

Before we can hit the road to start exploring, let's get a lay of the land. Alaska has very much adapted to RV travel over the years. There are numerous RV dump stations, free water fills, campgrounds with plug ins and extra-large parking spaces in many towns. We travel in a self-converted, fully off-grid, RAM ProMaster 3500 extended. As such, we don't often need these RV essentials but if you're traveling in a bigger rig with a black tank, you'll easily be able to find all the amenities to make your trip a breeze.

We were worried about road conditions after hearing so many stories about how bad the roads are. To eliminate that stress, we upgraded to extra beefy all terrain tires with some serious grip. These didn't prove to be a necessity, as most of the main roads in Alaska are in good condition. Locals drive around in all kinds of vehicles ranging from luxury sports cars and antique trucks to mom vans and hoopties. They all make it just fine. That's not to say it's all smooth sailing.

There is lots of road construction, miles and miles of unpaved or gravel roads in varying states of repair and if you want to get truly off grid into the wilderness, you never know what kind of road you'll be driving on. Plus, if you plan on staying into the fall, you'll need to be ready for snow because it can strike at any time. We are glad we made the tire upgrade anyway because we do a lot of winter exploring and depending on your style of adventure, this might be something to consider. But, if you're only going to be in Alaska around the summer solstice, June 21st, you'll be fine to drive on any good condition tires.

It's also smart to have safety gear in your rig. That ranges from recovery tracks to get out when you're stuck to extra fluids for your engine, a first aid kit, some basic tools and a heat source. Most cities and urban areas have great cell phone coverage, but on the highways between towns or off-grid, you might find yourself in a tricky situation without the means to call for help. Weather can change on a dime, breakdowns and accidents do happen and if you're not ready you'll regret it. Friends of ours equipped themselves with a satellite phone and ham radio as additional means of contacting support. If you're going deep, it's not a bad idea to have multiple means to call for assistance.

Speaking of weather, make sure you have some warm and waterproof clothing. Most people, including us, travel to Alaska in the summer. Alaskan summers can be gloriously hot. We had some beautiful days in the sun cooling down in our bathing suits by swimming in glacier fed water. We even got sunburnt on multiple occasions (speaking of which, let's add sunscreen to this prep list because the Alaskan sun is no joke). But more often than not, the weather required sweaters, coats, hats, wool socks and even gloves on occasion. There were days of dreary rain, where if you want to explore you need a weatherproof outfit or risk being cold and wet. It's one of those places that is usually perfect sleeping weather, cool to cold in the morning and evening but often glorious during the day. The further away you get from the solstice, the longest day of the year June 21st, the cooler the nights will be.

The final thing we did to prepare for Alaska was bulk purchase canned and non-perishable goods at lower 48 pricing (the lower 48 is what people in Alaska call the rest of the USA). Grocery prices in Alaska can be much higher than you're used to, so we purchase items like canned beans, tomatoes, pasta, rice, coffee, tea, nuts, seeds, protein bars, etc. to stock our shelves at prices we knew were good.

All the goods and products you see on the shelves in Alaska are shipped in from somewhere else and that adds to their cost. So, we cut out the middleman and imported some of our favorite foods and snacks ourselves. If you are driving through Canada, you'll need to check on which foods you are able to cross the border with and which you must leave at home (say goodbye to your house plants too).

Other than that, we were all set. After living on the road for two years you come to realize that if you don't have something, you can always find somewhere to buy it or have it shipped. If you've got your wallet, keys, phone, passport and a sense of adventure, you are good to go.

# Getting to Alaska

For most rigs, the obvious way to get to Alaska is to drive there. The ALCAN Highway is one of the most iconic in North America and is on many travelers' bucket lists. There are numerous guides about traversing the ALCAN, The Milepost being the most well-known. Unfortunately, this drive became impossible for a time when the Canadian border closed to all non-essential travel as a result of the COVID-19 global pandemic

At the beginning of the pandemic Canada closed its border to Americans and vice versa. Americans were slipping through the system by exercising their right to traverse Canada saying they were on their way to Alaska. For a while this worked and would have continued to work had it not been for some who lied about their intentions to go to Alaska and instead traveled in Canada. This angered many Canadians which lead to some steep fines for folks breaking the rules.

After that, the Canadian government closed this loophole and insisted that if you wanted to traverse Canada to get to Alaska you had to have work or residence in the 49th state.

And still, some folks figured out how to skirt around those rules, forging documents and rental agreements, so the requirements became even more strict and the border agents fiercer in keeping travelers out. That's when we decided it was the perfect time to drive through Canada.

Ill-advised as it sounds writing it now, we were working with a travel agency who wanted footage of Alaska to promote their package tours. We contacted Canada Border Services multiple times to make sure we had all the correct paperwork and thought we had covered all the bases and then some.

We showed up to the border hopeful that we would be on our way to Alaska that day, ready to drive the 2,152-miles in however few days they gave us (the lowest we heard was 3 days and the most was 7). After waiting four hours in line and being interrogated for two more, the agent let us know that he was never going to let us through. We would be the sixth people he had denied that day and there were at least five more cars behind us all waiting to get rejected too. After licking our wounds and feeling sorry for ourselves for a few days, we regrouped and started to look for alternate ways to get to Alaska.

The most common alternative is taking the passenger ferry from Bellingham to Whittier. This boat is operated by the state of Alaska and will transport you and your rig to Alaska in about seven days.

Over the last number of years, this option has become a less desirable one with most people preferring to make the drive themselves. Rumor has it, it was also becoming unprofitable, so the state sold off one of their boats which decreased the number of boats in operation. Then, surprise! Suddenly, the Canadian border closed making the ferry one of the only ways to get your car to Alaska and its popularity soared. The ferry implemented variable pricing much like the airlines do and voila, a cruise that used to cost $1,000 increased to $5,000. Not to mention that because there were fewer boats and more passengers, passages filled up quickly.

When we first looked in April there were only a few spots left and the price was $5,000 one day and $8,000 the next. You pay based on the length of your vehicle plus a cabin if you so desire. You are not permitted to sleep in your rig so you can either shell out for a room or tent camp on the top deck of the boat. Yes, you read that correctly. After getting denied at the border we checked the ferry again, there was zero availability until late September.

Afterwards we learned that some friends of ours found a loophole in the system we'll explain in greater detail later in this book. This made their time on the ferry longer, but they got to explore a coastal region of Alaska not accessible by any means but boat. It still cost them a pretty penny, but they had a lovely experience and were able to make it to Alaska in a year many could not.

The worst downside of the ferry is for your pet, if you have one. They must be crated for the entire ride, and you can only visit with them for twenty minutes every eight hours. There are also limited food options on board and the expensive cabins leave a lot to be desired. It's been coined the poor man's cruise because while you do get to see all that amazing coastal scenery folks pay mega bucks to experience on Alaskan cruise lines, you're sleeping in a tent eating cup-o-noodles.

With the ferry ride sold out, we started to panic. Would we be able to make it to Alaska that summer? There was talk of the Canadian border re-opening but the deadline just kept moving further and further out. It simultaneously felt like the perfect summer to be there with less tourists to enable us to get amazing shots for the travel agency and the worst summer with a global pandemic preventing us from getting there.

The only other option we could think of was shipping the van and flying to meet it. I started to look around for pricing and found TOTE Maritime. TOTE's entire business is moving goods and vehicles to and from Alaska out of Tacoma (just south of Seattle). Within minutes of speaking to the very friendly and knowledgeable booking agent, I had a quote and could be put on the very next sailing. They sail twice a week every week and it only takes four days for your vehicle to arrive in Anchorage. Our 21-foot vehicle was quoted at $4,700 which felt like a steal after seeing the ferry pricing. We used points for the flights which were surprisingly cheap, more points for a hotel which was surprisingly expensive, and just like that, we had our feet on the ground in Anchorage, Alaska.

By the time we were set to come back to the lower 48 after a summer of adventure, exploration and sightseeing, we decided to take TOTE back as well. We had a commitment in Washington we had to be back for and with the border just opening back up, we didn't want to risk driving all the way there just to find out we didn't have some random piece of paper we needed and not make it back in time. The ride back with TOTE is half the price of the way there but it takes seven days to arrive in Tacoma. This way we knew for sure we would make our very important meeting with the added benefit that the van saved over 4,600-miles of wear and tear. If you are interested in seeing all the sights along the drive to or from Alaska, you can check out our friends the Newstate Nomads who did an entire series on it.

As of now, the Canadian border is open to tourism for anyone who is fully vaccinated. That means you can make the drive in as much time as you want, if you meet the criteria. Who knows how the situation will change in the coming months or years so it's always a good idea to check with Canada Border Services before you plan your crossing into Canada and of course, you need a valid passport.

Whichever way you get to Alaska, all those miles and all the trouble getting there is totally worth it. We arrived in Alaska three days before the summer solstice. Leaving Seattle after the sun had set only to fly over fully lit mountain ranges that looked like they were straight out of another planet was insane. Landing and stepping outside only to realize it's fully bright even though it was midnight felt wild to say the least. We were 100% exhausted and 100% excited to start our adventure in this totally new to us land we'd always dreamed of.

# Cost of Travel in Alaska

While planning an Alaskan vacation, you also need to plan to have a stash of cash set aside. We heard from many locals how the price of tours has exponentially increased since they arrived only a few years ago. Something that used to cost $500, like visiting grizzly bears in Katmai National Park during the salmon run will now set you back $5,000. Set your expectations now that if you want to do the cool crazy stuff in Alaska, you're going to need to spend a few bucks.

There are of course acres of wild free Alaskan lands where you can camp, hike and explore without spending a dime. For us it was about finding a balance between the expensive excursions and the free ones. The luxury of traveling by van is that you can slowly make your way through the massive state and take your time in each town. You get to talk to people who've taken the expensive tours and find out firsthand if the cost is worth it.

When we first got to Alaska, it felt like we had to do everything all at once. We knew our time was limited and wanted to get it all in. We ended up spending money like crazy trying to eat, see, and experience it all.

Then we settled into a more comfortable routine of a few days relaxing and enjoying between bigger adventures. Near the end of our visit, we felt like the clock was running out and we went into overdrive again trying to fit it all in before we left. The fact of the matter is, the two months we spent in Alaska blew our budget straight out of the water. We are generally frugal but there's something about Alaska that just makes you want to throw it on the credit card and worry about it later.

Everything in Alaska is just a bit more expensive because almost everything has to be imported. Alaska doesn't grow bananas or manufacture computers. Most of the groceries on the shelf are shipped up or flown in. There is a cost of shipping everything into the state and an additional cost for getting those goods out of the major towns into the smaller ones. The further you are from city centers, the more costly goods become. We once spent $10 on a bag of potato chips in Copper Landing (crazy yes, but when the cravings hit…).

If you stock up and shop in main towns like Anchorage, Soldotna, Wasilla, and Fairbanks and stick to big name brand shops like Fred Meyers, Safeway, Walmart and the Alaskan Costco equivalent Three Bears (there's also a Costco in Anchorage), you can get comparable pricing on pantry goods.

Fresh fruits and vegetables are a bit more expensive in those areas but hugely more expensive elsewhere. Fresh produce was the biggest let down of our grocery shopping experience in Alaska. We spent way too much on items like strawberries, raspberries, and avocados only to find they weren't even very tasty. Because they travel so far to get there, they are either about to go bad the next day or never ripen and then go bad anyways. It's much safer to stick with green bananas, apples, potatoes, onions, cabbage, bell peppers and other fruits and vegetables that last well in the pantry. You'll feel much better about spending a bit more on food when it doesn't go bad before you get to eat it.

	If you extrapolate the cost of groceries, it's no surprise that eating out at restaurants will also be costly. Most entrees at restaurants, even average ones, are around $20. There are no $1 pizza slices (maybe we're just missing New York City) and even the cheap places don't feel all that cheap unless you're going to fast-food chains which are present in bigger cities (the Burger King app doesn't work in Alaska which means no deals – another craving hit). There were a few must eat items for us like locally caught salmon, halibut and fish and chips from the coast directly where the fish was caught.

Some folks love reindeer sausage, others are excited about fireweed honey. Of course, it's nice to eat out and sometimes, especially when you're in a hurry to get to your next destination, it's so much easier to pick something up than cook. But just like in any American city, it's less expensive to eat in than it is to eat out.

Another big expense on your Alaskan adventure is gas. Again, the closer you are to major city centers, the less you'll pay. The more remote the location, the more your tank will cost to fill. Want to drive to Prudhoe Bay? Expect to fill up at over $5 a gallon. The summer we visited the nation was experiencing uncharacteristically high gas prices so we figured our last fill up in Tacoma, Washington would be our least expensive all summer (and we could only fill a quarter of a tank because of shipping requirements). However, we found prices in Alaska to be comparable to states with more expensive gas in the lower 48.

We use a few apps to ensure we are getting the best prices on gas because often just a few miles down the road, you could find much better pricing. In Alaska the only app that worked for us was GasBuddy which was very helpful all over the state to find the best pricing and also get discounts on gas from 5 to 10 cents a liter.

We often use GetUpside in the lower 48 but it only worked at Holiday gas stations in Alaska, mainly around Anchorage. Safeway and Fred Meyers have great gas discounts for shoppers who rack up points on their club cards by buying groceries. We've swiped and saved upwards of 40 cents a gallon at these grocery store pumps. For some reason I had this idea that gas stations would be sparce and we should fill up whenever there was an opportunity.

   Although this is true for the most remote highways in Alaska like the Dalton, normally you're never more than 100 miles to the nearest gas station or town. Using gas price apps and driving those few extra miles to get a deal can really make a difference on your wallet, but of course, if you're running on empty, fill up wherever you can.

   Going into it knowing you're going to need a few extra dollars to enjoy your stay is the best way to operate. Heck, the least expensive way to just arrive in Alaska is going to cost you hundreds of dollars in gas.

This is not a destination for thrifty travel. But by far the least expensive way to travel around Alaska is by camper van. We needed a hotel room for four nights while we waited for our van to make the TOTE boat ride so did some research into options. Hotel rooms were $400 a night and Airbnb's around $200. Imagine that even sixty-six days at an average RV park for $30 a night would be almost $2,000. Boondocking with apps like iOverlander literally saves you thousands of dollars. Plus, you have a kitchen on board to cook your own meals and save cash that way too.

# The Truth About Alaskan Roads

Honestly, they aren't that bad. We were worried that all the roads would be terrible, full of frost heaves and potholes. I won't lie, some of the roads were terrible, but most of them, especially the main highways, are in very good shape.

For as large as the state of Alaska is, 424 million acres to be exact, there aren't that many roads. Including forestry roads there are only 14,336-miles of public roads in Alaska. That leaves many acres of Alaska only accessible by airplane and towns only accessible by boat. Acre upon acre of untouched wilderness. That's the reason many people come to Alaska, to see this natural, wild land, untouched by humans.

The main arteries that flow through Alaska all connect back through Anchorage in one way or another. Anchorage is the heart of the wild and so stopping through and stocking up between adventures is very easy. South of Anchorage you have the Seward Highway that connects to the Sterling Highway to take you all the way down to Homer.

Along the way you can take side trips to Whittier, Moose Pass, and the Kenai Fjords National Park. You'll have to drive this same route back north to loop back through Anchorage before setting out on your next adventure because there is only one way in and one way out. This might seem boring but somehow the view going the opposite way was always a nice surprise to us. It's an entirely different vantage point and you'll likely see the road in a whole new way the second time you drive it.

The highways north of Anchorage felt like a giant triangle. Along the bottom you have the Glenn highway that takes you through Glacier View and Glennallen. From there you can head south to Valdez on the Richardson or take the triangle up to Fairbanks on the Sterling. The other side of the massive triangle heads north from Anchorage through Denali National Park to Fairbanks. From Fairbanks, you can head north to Prudhoe Bay on the Dalton highway, the start of the Pan American Highway and the gateway to the Arctic.

Map from: https://www.alaskacenters.gov/trip-planning/travel/road

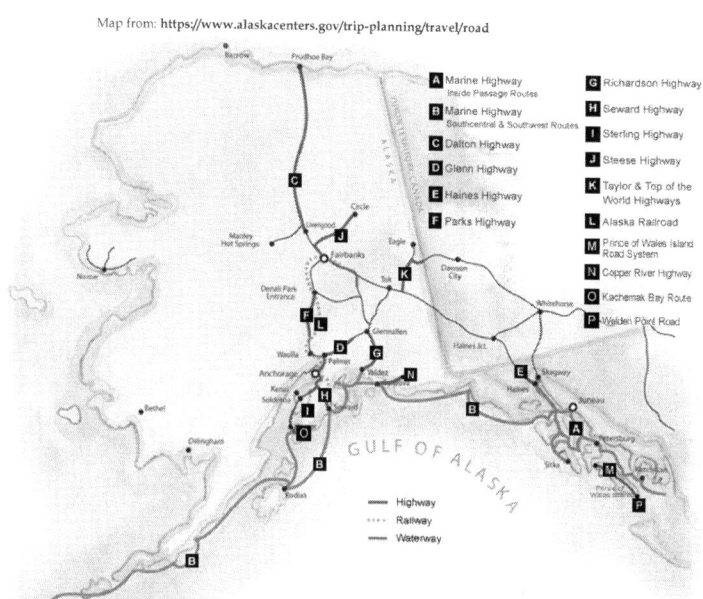

As you can see, most of the state is uncharted territory. Many locals use four-wheelers, also known as ATVs and snow-machines, also known as snowmobiles, to navigate the roadless wilderness. We took a four-wheeling adventure out of Glacier View on the Glenn highway with a fifty-year Alaskan local.

He took us deep into the tundra, twenty miles off the main roads into stunning untouched countryside. Even as we stood at the top of a rolling hill nestled between mountains eating wild blueberries right from the vine, we knew we'd barely scratch the surface of what Alaska had to offer. Our guide pointed across to the base of the next climbing hill and proclaimed, "there could be twenty moose in there and you would never know, the grass is head-high".

For the most part, anything listed as a highway was, during our visit, in good repair. Folks will warn you about the frost heaves and if you're driving the ALCAN highway (the Alaska Canada highway that takes you through Canada to get to Alaska) they will be marked with pink little flags at the side of the road. Frost heaves are essentially cracks and shifts in the pavement that create road hazards after the ice has thawed. Lower your speed and treat it like a speed bump - you'll be fine.

Because of the deep, long, cold, winters in Alaska the roads are constantly under construction. Many of the highways are two lanes with areas for passing so when construction happens there is generally a pilot car that will lead you through a stretch of one lane highway. We didn't notice that much construction until we started getting north of the Denali highway. As we rolled closer to Fairbanks, the roads got increasingly worse, and the patches of construction got increasingly longer.

The Denali and Dalton highways are in and of themselves an attraction as well as a roadway. It's roads like this that folks from the lower 48 are weary of and for good reason. They are bumpy, loud, and jarring. Potholes and washboard sections last for miles, there is zero cell phone service, and only one option - keep driving. The views along these routes are spectacular and there are endless pull-offs for a night or twelve in the wild. But be warned, these roads both have a reputation for cracking windshields and popping tires. If you plan to travel on them, you need to have a spare tire and the ability to change it yourself. There are times when you won't see another car for hours, so you need to be prepared to be self-sufficient. How convenient you live in a tiny home on wheels!

The greatest hazard on any Alaskan road, whether you're downtown or in the sticks, is wildlife. Deer and moose are your biggest threats as they will total your vehicle. We saw the remnants of a car that tangoed with a moose - it was not pretty. You can buy a deer whistle for the hood of your car that emits a noise, undetectable by you, designed to deter animals from jumping out into the road. These big mammals like to come out at dusk and dawn, a relative concept in Alaska when the sun is out all day. Always stay alert and keep an eye on the side of the road for any movement or the flash of reflective eyes.

Finally, don't forget to watch speed limits. Roads quickly drop their speed as you get closer to towns and cops are excited to take advantage of that. We got one speeding ticket during our visit and felt more like we were being singled out for having out of state plates than having done anything wrong. That's all hearsay but don't say we didn't warn you. As lawless as Alaska feels, it's not.

Once you get off the main arteries of the Alaskan highway system, the road quality does diminish but not so much that you're going to destroy your car. Of course, you can get into some gnarly backcountry but all the spots we have listed in this guide are easy to traverse and didn't cause any damage to our rig. I can't guarantee anything, but if you're a good driver and know how to maneuver your vehicle, you shouldn't have any issues driving in Alaska.

# Internet Connectivity and Cell Phone Signal

Since we do all our work on the internet, it's important for us to be able to get connected. Alaska has all the same carriers as the lower 48 plus GCI which is exclusive to Alaska. GCI has the best coverage and although Sprint and T-Mobile have roaming agreements with GCI their coverage is weak and you'll be roaming basically the whole time you're there. If you want to get the best possible shot of service, you could get a prepaid sim card from GCI, but we didn't find that necessary.

The next best coverage is with AT&T so before we arrived, we set ourselves up with their router plan with 100 GB for $55 a month. We put that sim card into a mobile router we got from Mobile Must Haves called the Full Time RV and Boat Bundle. Between this and our Verizon cell phones, Verizon having the next best service, we had connectivity most of the time.

Of course, there is a lot of Alaska that doesn't have any service. Heck there's a lot of Alaska with no roads, why would there be internet way out there? But if you're in a town, even a small one, you're almost guaranteed to have at least some connectivity. The further you get off-grid, the less chance you'll be able to get online.

Along the highways in Alaska, you generally flow in and out of service as you drive through towns. On the more remote highways like Denali and Dalton you'll have no service for long stretches. If you're worried about breaking down and not having connection, don't. Most roads are busy enough, so a helpful stranger is just a car or two away. However, on other more remote highways that wait could turn into a few hours. If you want the backup, you could get a satellite phone for just those kinds of situations. There's a high upfront cost for the hardware, but the monthly plans aren't crazy.

In some spots we would have just enough connectivity to send texts, in others we could upload full YouTube videos. If we really needed to be online, we'd go to more populated areas, simple as that. The whole point of being in Alaska is to experience the great outdoors, so if you don't have the internet for a while, look up from your phone and go explore.

# Wild Camping in Alaska

Alaska is one of the most boondocking friendly states in all of America. Of those miles and miles of untouched lands, most are public and available for camping. The general rule in Alaska is that if you can clear the road and are parked in a safe location that won't obstruct other drivers, you're fine to stay the night. People would rather you rest and drive safely, or pull off when the weather is bad, than cause an accident.

We mainly trusted iOverlander, personal recommendations and our intuition to find places to camp. iOverlander has many spots listed all over the state. Take one look at the map and any anxieties about finding free camping will disappear.

There are also tons of campgrounds, both public campgrounds without fees and private campgrounds with fees. Many of these are also listed on iOverlander but sites like Campendium are also a great resource. We only paid to camp two nights out of our sixty-six days in Alaska plus three days in the National Park. The first time was because we were having an electrical problem that caused us to completely run out of house power.

We pulled up to the campground in Bird Ridge along the Seward highway (which looked more like a parking lot for a motel than a campground) and were offered a spot right away. It was $30 to plug in for any length of time so we used the day to charge our batteries and fix the issue with our electrical system. The problem turned out to be a bad crimp on a wire which was simple to repair with the tools we always keep on board.

The second campground we paid for was $20 on the Spit in Homer, Alaska. We were traveling with friends who had been there before and believed there was nowhere free or stealth to camp in the area. We dropped our cash in a giant metal fish and enjoyed a stroll and dinner on the pier. The next morning, we ran into Drifter Journey, some more van life friends, who found a stealthy parking lot even closer to the action than the campground. We spent the next three nights in that parking lot without issue (we will provide GPS links for all our spots in an index at the end of the book).

If you decide not to drive to Alaska yourself, you can rent an RV or other vehicle to live in while you're there. In the summer of 2021, the entire state was experiencing a rental car shortage. Prices were sky high for the inventory they had, and the private rental market boomed. We met a couple who rented a red minivan for the week and were living out of that because every RV in the state was rented out. If you're planning on going this route, make sure you book early or consider some interesting alternatives like living out of a U-Haul, rental car or renting from an individual on sites like Outdoorsy, the Airbnb of vans and RVs.

No mater what you're driving, the majority of the camping spots we share in this guide are accessible to all rigs. We'll let you know if the road is steep or the space narrow but for the most part, you can just pull right on into any of these locations in any rig. Of course, the deeper you want to go, the less likely a giant RV is to take you there.

Free camping is the least expensive thing you'll do in Alaska so you should get comfortable with seeking out known locations or learn to find all the hidden spots for yourself. Knowing you can't really get in trouble for it, makes it all the more fun to get out and explore. If you're worried about accidently camping on private land, you can download the onXoffroad or onXhunt maps to see the land designations around you including public lands. For us it's most fun to camp in the middle of nowhere surrounded by nature, fresh air and wild animals. But to get there, we have to start with some urban stealth camping in the seventy fourth biggest city in America.

# Anchorage

The largest town in Alaska by far is Anchorage with just under 300,000 residents (the next largest town is the capital city of Juneau with 32,000 residents). This is where your van will arrive if you ship with TOTE. This is also where every highway in Alaska leads to, for good reason. Because of its size you will find all the best prices and the widest variety of goods here. There is practically every brand name store you'd expect to see in the lower 48 from Best Buy to REI, Burger King to Outback Steakhouse. Make sure to stock up on groceries and buy any consumer goods you might need.

Anchorage is also a great place to dine out. There are endless restaurants of every variety and in every price range. We picked up a local coupon book at the Barns and Nobel called Northern Lights. They keep it behind the counter because it's so valuable. For $55 you get discounts at 200 different business in Alaska ranging from free appetizers at the nicest restaurants in Anchorage, to two-for-one excursions worth hundreds of dollars.

After running around all day doing errands, there are several very nice parks and waterfront trails to explore. The Tony Knowles Coastal Trail is an eleven-mile paved walkway perfect for biking, dog walking, long boarding, roller blading and whatever else you can think of. We picked up the trail multiple times from various entry points and each time were happy to be immediately immersed in nature right next to the big city. We even rented a tandem bike to explore the trail further with our dog Paco running beside us. Earthquake Park was another favorite of ours with so much history of the massive quake and resulting tsunami that reshaped Alaska on Good Friday in 1964.

There are a few established campgrounds in the city. We used one for three hours trying to charge our batteries when we were having the electrical issue we mentioned earlier (the guy cut us a deal and only charged us $10 instead of the nightly rate of $30). But for us, wild and free is always better. We ended up multiple times in a neighborhood that was under construction with massive, multi-million-dollar homes. At the end of the block is a popular neighborhood park with porta-potties, baseball fields and connection to the waterfront trail.

You can't sleep in the parking lot for the park as it is closed and locked at 10pm sharp. But right at the corner of that street there are no overnight parking rules (there are none anywhere in Alaska unless otherwise posted). If you're following the posted signs, you're good to stay the night.

When urban camping, especially in neighborhoods, there are a few tried and true rules to abide by. Arrive late - we try to arrive after dark but that's pretty much impossible in Alaska. Leave early - you don't have to wake up at the crack of dawn, but you don't want to linger too long either. There are all kinds of places where you can hang out during the day in the city (parks, coffee shops, store parking lots, libraries, gyms, etc.) so there's no need to stay in a neighborhood potentially catching the eye of an unwelcoming or concerned homeowner. To avoid their eye even further, don't set up camp like you might in the woods - leave the camp chairs and outdoor grill for another day.

Just outside of the sprawling city of Anchorage you enter Chugach State Park. This massive National Park offers opportunity for recreation over 495,204 acres. A popular high just twenty minutes from downtown is Flattop Mountain.

This 1.5-mile 1,215-foot elevation gain hike is a workout to say the least, but you are rewarded with sprawling views of Anchorage and the surrounding area. Slightly lesser known, less trafficked and apparently easier is Rendezvous Peak (3.1-mile 1,397-feet elevation) which offers equally breathtaking views without the crowd fame brings.

To the north is Eklutna Lake, the winding uphill drive to get there is totally worth it. You can camp either at the base of the sixteen-mile drive outside Thunderbird Falls (a very short very easy hike to a still kind of distant waterfall) or on the side of the road twisting and turning up the mountain. When you get to the recreation area at the top of the hill, you can continue hiking up to Twin Peaks or rent a kayak and cruise along the seven-mile-long lake nestled in a valley of mountains and glaciers. We did both and loved every minute of it. Unfortunately, you can't camp for free at the top. There is a paid campground, but just a few miles down the road you can park at the side of the road for free.

In Anchorage we found the best showers at Planet Fitness. If you don't have a membership, it will cost you $10 for a day pass with an out of state driver's license. The Planet Fitness next to REI worked best for us as some had higher prices or no discount for out of state folks.

We really should just pay for a membership since we utilize their showers all the time, but we didn't want to sign up in Alaska because in order to cancel a Planet Fitness membership, you need to walk into your home club and cancel in person. We couldn't take that risk since we weren't sure when we would be back to Alaska (probably sooner than later because we really did fall in love).

The first four days we were in Anchorage we were true tourists. Having flown into the city from Seattle with our van Olive on a boat heading north to meet us, we took a cab to our hotel and crashed at midnight with the sun and the city still wide awake. We woke up the next morning to a dreary overcast day, threw on our coats and got to exploring. Because we didn't have our kitchen, we had to eat out for breakfast, lunch and dinner every day, something we almost never do. This was before we had our magical coupon book so we were paying full price for everything. It hurt, but we did find a few favorites that we would highly recommend.

For the obligatory fancy meal in Anchorage, we went to 49th State Brewing and sat up on their rooftop patio overlooking the waterfront. There is always a wait at this spot.

We signed up when the list was only 2 hours long and even though the food is slightly overpriced, it was tasty, and you can enjoy the best view in town. When we found out they were in the coupon book after the fact, I kicked myself.

Up next is El Green Go's, the best Mexican food in all of Alaska. They smoke all their meats in a giant BBQ on site but can make everything on their menu vegan if you want. In front of their shipping container style building, they have outdoor seating at patio tables. The founders are fine dining chefs who decided to branch off on their own, so you know the food is top notch. We ate here three times during our tour of Alaska and made sure it was our last meal before leaving the 49th state. Everything is fresh, vibrant and reasonably priced, plus the whole staff are incredibly friendly. It's our kind of hang out.

Finally, you're going to need a good cup of coffee eventually so why not try Side Street Espresso. This hole in the wall is run by an adorable elderly couple who must be exhausted because they are on their feet hustling all day to keep up with the constant flow of caffeine seekers. I kid you not, the chai latte I had from here is the best chia latte I've had in my entire life. Frankie said the same thing about his caramel latte. They are closed Sunday and Monday which was a huge disappointment on day two when we tried to go back, but we did return every time we were in the city and were never disappointed again.

    We really did enjoy our time in Anchorage but, a city is a city no matter what state you're in. It's the wilderness we came to Alaska for, so let's get into it.

# Seward Highway & Girdwood

We had a hard time deciding our route to tackle the biggest state in America (Alaska is 665,384 square miles to be exact, that's almost 400,000 more square miles than Texas if you were wondering). Did we want to head north first as Fairbanks has the hottest summers and the Arctic Circle gets cold more quickly than the Kenai. Or would we rather spend the hottest months of the summer in the coastal towns? We ended up letting fate and our friends decide the route.

We had plans to travel to the Arctic Circle with Adaptive Humanity who in June were still finishing their van build in Florida. Then we kept hearing Seward was the place to be for the 4$^{th}$ of July, so we decided south first, north second.

That meant our first journey from Anchorage was along the Seward Highway. We spend our first night out of the city sleeping at the side of the highway near Beluga Point less than twenty miles from the city but with a completely different vibe.

What we didn't know until much later in our trip is that this is where the famed Alaskan tidal wave rolls. Every twelve hours, you can watch or join in as a dozen or so committed surfers paddle out to try and catch the only wave they'll see until the next tide swell. T A Surf Company offers tours and can hook you up with all the gear and knowledge you need to get out there.

Or you can watch from the comfort of the roadside pull offs. I can't give you an exact location because the surfers move up and down the Turnagain Arm depending on the many factors determining the location of the bore tide (look for the pull-off with the most cars and surfboards). But what I know for sure is that it's a very cool event to watch. The surfers seem exhausted when they finish riding and thirty minutes after the wave passes you, the waters swell and the beluga whales swim by. We didn't realize the phenomena until we were hanging out talking about the wave with some friends who had just ridden it when suddenly, a whale crested right behind them. We were all amazed and whipped out our cameras to capture the magic. We later learning this happens every day as the whales follow the tide, so cool.

Moving further down the Seward highway, you come to a town called Girdwood. Girdwood is most well-known for the ski village Alyeska that calls it home. But we loved Girdwood simply for being Girdwood. It is so quaint and friendly. They have America's best laundromat according to some obscure vote we're not quite sure the validity of, but it was a nice place. We did our laundry here at least three times as the showers are hot and clean, and the Wi-Fi is fast too.

Girdwood also has several cute restaurants and coffee shops. We didn't frequent too many of these but did enjoy a nightcap and dessert at Spoons (BOGO from our coupon book). The grocery store in town is very small and overpriced but you shouldn't need it with your stocked fridge having come from either Anchorage in the north or Soldotna in the south. They do have a lovely farmers market there every Sunday and honestly the whole town just felt welcoming.

You can camp for free for up to 72 hours in the parking spaces provided by the city surrounding the town square (right across from the laundromat). There are bathrooms available in the various establishments in town and a porta-potty for anyone to use. If you venture to the trailheads just north of town towards Alyeska, most places say no overnight camping, but we pushed our luck twice and were just fine.

Alyeska is a very posh resort with a tram you can ride in the summer or winter to get to the top of the mountain. The tram ride is $35 per person or if you're feeling adventurous you can hike up the mountain, grab a beer at the top and ride it back down for free. The tram was cool and all, but the hike sounds like the better experience plus you still get to ride it down. The other famous hike in town is probably permanently shut down after two people died. The hand tram was once the only way to cross the river along the Winner Creek trail. User operated means there's a chance for user error and after tragedy struck twice, it was shut down, the hike it still lovely and wooded.

Crow Pass is another popular hike in the area not for the faint of heart. We were going to attempt it but the day we had set aside for it we ran out of propane with a half-cooked breakfast in the pan and had to head to Anchorage to get the tank refilled (there are propane fills at most gas station however, our tank was being weird and would not fill). That's one thing about van life and full-time travel, you have to be able to roll with the punches.

If you're not familiar with the topography of Alaska, you're in for a treat. Alyeska isn't the only mountain you can hope to ski, snowboard, paraglide, hike or downhill bike. As you can see, there are literally mountain ranges everywhere. From the Aleutian Range in the south to the Brooks Range in the north, it's almost guaranteed you'll always have a mountain in your line of sight. Of course, most of these mountains are inaccessible. There are only seven established ski resorts in the state. Valdez invented heliboarding for just that reason, no infrastructure needed, just get dropped off at the top by a helicopter and ride your way down.

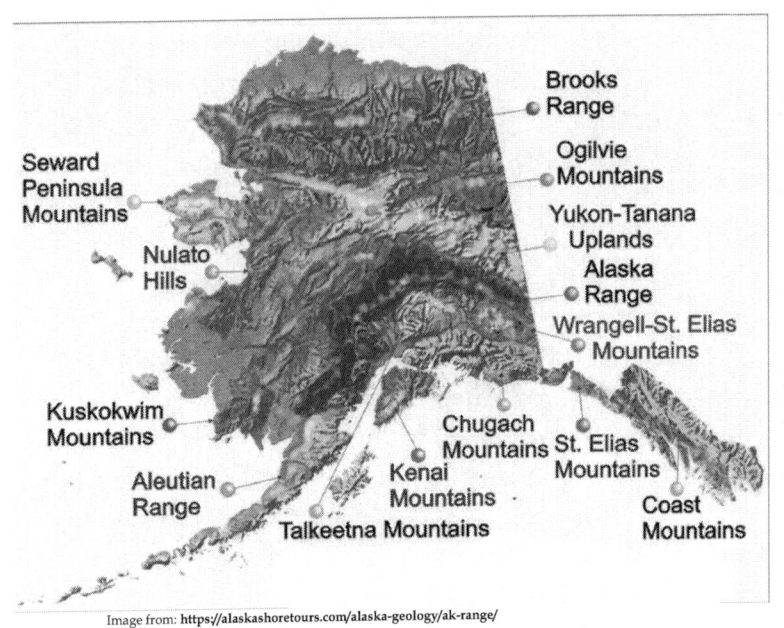

Image from: https://alaskashoretours.com/alaska-geology/ak-range/

We visited Girdwood three times during our Alaskan adventure. Once on our way to Homer, then on our way back to Anchorage and finally it was our last stop before boarding the plane to return to the lower 48. It has a special place in our heart and to top it all off we saw a black bear walking across the street in the middle of town. Girdwood is amazing.

Still technically in Anchorage, twenty minutes east of Girdwood, you'll reach the Portage Glacier area. This once massive glacier has receded dramatically over the last number of years. The entire lake used to be a glacier, now you need a boat tour just to see it. We embarked on this group tour with a two-for-one deal from our coupon book and a same day booking. We enjoyed the scenery and learning about our impact on the changing climate while watching the glacier calve. In places like Alaska the changes are so dramatic and in your face it's hard to ignore the sad truth of it all. Many glaciers have then-and-now side by side photos near them to showcase just how noticeable the difference has become.

Next to Portage Glacier we found a sneaky little pull off that looked like it was once under construction as the work portables were still there. But as work seemed to be at a standstill, we pulled our rig right up to a stunning lake with a mountain jutting out the back side of it (the cover of this book). Pretty spectacular. We gave the spot to a friend later in the summer and it seems work had restarted, and you can no longer camp there, but we have provided the coordinates in the Where We Slept section just in case it's open when you go. There were several spots nearby so if this one is closed, keep an eye out for pull offs on either side of the road.

# Whittier

To the east of the Seward highway, past Portage Glacier, you'll arrive at the tunnel to Whittier. A town once cut off from the rest of Alaska and only accessible by boat. In 1943 a massive tunnel was opened to connect the port town to the rest of Alaska by train to transport goods. It wasn't until 2000 that cars were allowed to make the drive as well. Now they have a very structured and orderly operation that moves cars and trains into and out of Whitter through this one lane 2.5-mile tunnel.

Take note of the schedule to make sure you're not waiting too long for your turn. Every thirty minutes one side of the tunnel is released and starting from $13 round trip, you get to drive through the first tunnel designed for -40-degree Fahrenheit temperatures and 150 mile an hour wind. Even though it's insanely cold, Whittier is the only deep-water port in Alaska that doesn't freeze over in the winter; probably why it was worth all the trouble to build the tunnel in the first place.

Luckily, we visited in the summer so didn't have to worry about the winds smashing our windshield to bits. We were greeted with a surprisingly beautiful port town. This might be due to the fact we got some glorious weather while we were there and there is nothing more beautiful than an Alaskan port town in the sunshine. Alaskan's say, Whittier is Shittier, but to us, there was something charming about this city. The wooden boardwalk, the many boats bobbing in the harbor, the sleepy feeling, it was quaint.

We had some amazing food both at China Sea Restaurant as well as at Wild Catch Café. Both were pricy, but what can you expect from a town so cut off from the rest of the world. The Hotel was also recommended as a great place to catch a bite but when we walked in, the place was slammed, and they admitted people had been waiting 2+ hours for their food. A common theme in many restaurants in Alaska in 2021 was a severe shortage of staff. Some restaurants didn't even open this year because they couldn't find reliable cooks, servers and the like largely because of US Canada border restrictions.

Another interesting Whittier fact is that 70% of its residents live in the same pink, high-rise building. We heard that everyone lived in the same building so when we rolled into town and the first structure we saw was a giant concrete building that looked like it was falling apart, I was shocked so many people lived there. Turns out though, that haunted looking building hasn't been in use in years, thankfully.

When you drive into Whittier, the very first righthand turn you can make is Portage Pass Trail. After a short potholed road, you'll reach the trailhead, where I'd venture to guess you'd be fine to camp for the night if you wanted to (we got swarmed with mosquitos on our way out so be warned). The hike itself offers stunning views, at a cost. It's completely uphill for the first section to a stunning overlook of Whitter on one side and Portage Glacier on the other. Then it's straight downhill the other way to a rocky beach where you can sunbathe with ice burgs floating in the water and have the most direct view of Portage Glacier without taking the boat cruise. This is all well and good except at this point, you have to turn around, hike back up a mountain and then back down to the parking area. It's only 4.2 miles and 1,433 feet in elevation which wasn't the hardest hike we did in Alaska, but it wasn't easy either. Well worth it for the bucket list view.

Our favorite thing to do in Whittier by far was the jet ski tour we booked before coming to Alaska. Frankie worked at a boat jet ski rental in the Gulf of Florida for many years so when he heard about a tour that would get him back on a jet ski in Alaska, he was super excited. The major difference between Florida and Alaska jet skiing adventures is the weather. In Florida it's bikini central with sunscreen and sunglasses on deck. In Alaska it's full dry-suits, helmets and gloves. The company we worked with, Glacier Jet Ski Adventures, hooked us up with all the gear we needed. After a brief safety lesson, we were off. Never having ridden a jet ski before, I was given a quick tutorial on how the machine worked but honestly, it was so simple I barely needed it.

We cruised at speeds upwards of 50 miles an hour into the Prince William Sound and then off into Blackstone Bay to see multiple massive glaciers. Along the way we saw tons of wildlife and waterfalls while having so much fun operating the machines. We would stop from time to time to hear some history about the area or to get up close to the action for some epic photos. It was truly a one-of-a-kind experience and affirmed why the pricy tours cost so much - they are incredible adventures.

Whittier is also the port town where the ferry lands if you're taking the budget cruise from Bellingham. I'd imagine that after a week at sea, you might be feeling like you need to get out of Whittier as quickly as possible. But I'd urge you to stay for at least one night. The best place to boondock in Whittier is at the end of a three-mile road up to the side of a winding cliffside. It's a beautiful place to stay with sweeping views of the harbor and surrounding glaciers.

But eventually you'll need to leave town since there's no real grocery store and after you've wandered the harbor, gone for a hike and had some good food, you'll be ready to take the tunnel back. The people working the tunnel are extremely nice and twice made sure we weren't going to miss the crossing. Once after our hike at Portage Pass, they came over and inquired if we were heading back because if we were, we had to go now. We weren't but it was nice of them to look out for us. On the way out of town, we raced from our campsite at the complete opposite side of Whittier trying to make it and thought for sure we were late. Well, they saw us coming and kept the gate open just long enough for us to drive through, so amazing. After a lovely time in Whittier, we were ready explore the rest of Alaska.

# Seward

Known as the RV capital city of Alaska and 4th of July party town, Seward has an interesting history too. After the 9.2 magnitude Good Friday earthquake in 1964, the Seward waterfront was completely reshaped. And by that, I mean the majority of it was swallowed into the sea. The waterfront was deemed unfit for building homes or other structures so the entirety of it was converted into RV parks. Not the fancy, tree lined RV parks of your dreams. Gravel parking lots with RV after RV jammed together. It didn't look like a good time to us and apparently the prices have skyrocketed in recent years.

Just ten minutes outside of town, in the runoff of Exit Glacier, is a riverbed with unlimited spots for free camping. There is a local guy here who collects and cuts up driftwood to sell for campfires so pick up a bundle if you can. We traded him a fishing rod for a car full of wood - he was an incredibly nice guy. We arrived here a few days before the 4th of July, it was already busy but there was still tons of space to spread out.

It was very cool to be on the rocky riverbed surrounded by snowcapped, goat roaming hills. It did get loud at night, especially as festivities ramped up for the holiday. There were fireworks and gunshots into all hours of the night, but who wouldn't be excited to celebrate America by screaming happy Independence Day at 3am before shooting off a mortar?

The entire town of Seward ramped up for the holiday. It was busy everywhere with American flag decorated streets, festivals, full RV parks and endless fishing charters showing off their catch of the day at the harbor. Restaurants were full, sidewalks were bustling, the atmosphere was light, happy, and patriotic. We spend the afternoon wandering and ended up eating lunch at a spot I wouldn't rush back to. Then we headed back to our riverbed camp spot to wait for the fireworks starting at midnight.

If we were to go back to Seward, I would avoid it on the 4th of July. I think it was just all too much for us and from the sounds of it, the most touristy place to be that day, hence the overabundance of RVs. Everywhere in the state will be celebrating Independence Day so there's no need to go to *the* place to be. We later heard of an annual tradition to launch cars off a cliff and watch them blowup near Glacier View, that sounds like a much cooler way to spend 4th of July if you ask me, but to each their own.

The things we did love about Seward were more on the outskirts of town. First up is an old railway car that's been converted into a sweet hangout spot and coffee shop. 13 Ravens Coffee & Books has great brews and in the adjacent railway car is The Smoke Shack with delicious Mexican inspired fare. You can also explore Kenai Fjords National Park either by foot or by sea. Drive northwest of town past the riverbed camp spot and you'll be welcomed to the Exit Glacier Nature Center, a spinoff of the Kenai Fjords National Park. Here you can either take a leisurely stroll to see the glacier from a far or an extreme hike that allows you to walk on the glacier via the Harding Icefield Trailhead. Feeling exhausted from the 4am gunshots and celebratory screams of "Happy 4th of July" we opted for the former.

There are multiple tour companies offering guided half or full day boat cruises from Seward to explore Kenai Fjords National Park. Since the majority of the National Park is only accessible by boat, this is the best way to experience it. Seward is also known for its fishing charters if this is something you're interested in.

In terms of supplies and refitting your rig, there's a big Safeway as you're entering town that has reasonable prices. There are also many free waters fill locations because of all the RV parks and campgrounds. Frankie and I filled up twice while we were here, once at a campground on the edge of town and once at one of the many downtown RV parks - both were free. At the downtown campgrounds you'll also find a coin operated shower. Frankie had an amazing hot shower, mine was freezing cold. At the time, only one of the ladies' showers had hot water and I got unlucky. As I stood in the freezing cold water, I watched the steam bellow from the stall next to mine while the only steam in my shower was coming from my ears.

For us the best part of Seward wasn't downtown, it was the wild camping on the outskirts. It was nice to come into civilization and explore, but it always felt to amazing to get back to camp, start a fire and relax for the evening. We had friends visit this same camping spot weeks later who said they basically had the whole place to themselves. Unless you enjoy a rowdy time, steer clear of Seward on major holidays.

The drive to and from the main highway toward Seward, number 9 on Google Maps, is littered with cute towns and amazing hikes. I wouldn't suggest buying groceries along this route as prices are sky high and there's nary a fresh vegetable in sight, but the coffee was reasonably priced, and the scenery is spectacular. A few hikes we dogeared but didn't have time for are Lost Lake Trail, Lower Lake Trail, Johnson Pass Trail and Moose Pass is also a favorite hangout with a wonderful boondocking option on iOverlander. Since this road is the only way in and out of Seward you have two opportunities to explore along the way so it's worth checking some of them out. Even if you don't, it's a beautiful drive winding along pristine lakes, rolling hills, and forests.

# Cooper Landing

As we continue our journey on the Seward Highway towards Homer, we reach what some might think of as a passthrough town. We ended up circling Cooper Landing for many days coming in and out of the forest. The USDA Forest Service has several dispersed camping areas in the Chugach National Forest listed on their website. Before we set out, I marked these all on my map just in case we needed a place to sleep or wanted to take a hike we could camp at. Most of these locations surround the town of Cooper Landing. We ended up finding our favorite camping spot in all of Alaska here from a local who gave us *his* favorite spot in confidence. We've since shared it with a few friends and now we will share it with you with the utmost trust and understanding that we've got to keep it clean and keep it quiet. Please do not share this site on any camp sharing app as we promised to do the same. It's a favorite for locals and we'd hate to blow it up.

This spot was our favorite for good reason. Well off the beaten path you'll have a long drive on an okay dirt road. Pass two of the major trailheads in the area then come to the end of the road that's closed with a gate.

Turn left and you're at the waterfront. To the right is a damn that did nothing while we were there (except I suppose hold back millions of gallons of water so, that's awesome). To the right you've got a big open space to choose from. The dirt looks hard packed all the way down to the water, but we did get stuck when we drove too close to the waves so keep that in mind. You'll have no cell phone service but some of the most gorgeous days on the water followed by breathtaking sunsets and peaceful nights sleeping. We came here twice, once on our way south and again on our way north and loved it both times.

We didn't find an actual downtown of Cooper Landing. It's more like several shops and businesses spread out along the highway. We ended up at Wildman's multiple times as they have a bit of everything. Bathrooms, showers, a couple of laundry machines, snacks, a deli counter and lots of ice cream flavors to choose from. We did laundry, bought a $10 bag of chips and hung out in the parking lot for many hours working and getting connected back to the world via the internet. The best deal here by far is the ice cream. It was something like $3 for a single scoop that was bigger than my head.

We were also able to book a last-minute two-for-one river rafting cruise we found in our coupon book with Alaskan River Adventures. There are several river adventure companies for wildlife viewing and fishing alike as Cooper Landing runs beside the shores of the Kenai River. We saw more eagles along this three-hour rafting trip than I have in my entire life combined. We also saw a black bear, a beaver, a porcupine, golden eagles and so many different types of birds and ducks I couldn't begin to name or identify them all. The cruise was a real pleasure and they set you up with a very sexy full army green waterproof fisherman's outfit complete with a hood so when it started to rain it, we kept warm and dry.

We made friends with the folks sitting next to us on the raft and they suggested we go out for dinner at the best restaurant in Cooper Landing, the Kenai Princess Wildness Lodge. We enjoyed a delicious three course dinner with fancy cocktails to book. My only suggestion here is that if you take the evening boat cruise, which is recommended as you're more likely to see wildlife late afternoon, you'll need to boogie over to the restaurant quickly because we got there within thirty minutes of closing and were the last table in there.

On our way westward, we stayed at one of the free government managed campsites at Watson Lake. This spot was quite nice featuring a boat launch into a lily pad laden waterway, three big camp spots and a pit toilet. The only problem was the mosquitos. We got swarmed as soon as we got out of the van. After a quick trip to the bathroom for ourselves and Paco, we headed in for the night killing the few mosquitos that followed us in. Thinking we got them all, we headed to bed only to be woken up an hour later to the dreaded sound of a mosquito buzzing by our heads.

Throughout the night, we were woken up almost every hour to kill another mosquito. Finally, we figured out they were climbing in through our roof hatch which is remarkable considering they had to find the entrance, go over the plastic casing, down around the blackout curtain, under and out the decorative shroud to get in. Before coming to Alaska, we heard tales of mosquitos the size of hummingbirds, so we were expecting Jurassic Park sized bugs to divebomb us at every turn. As cool or terrifying as that sounds, it wasn't the case at all.

The mosquitos in Alaska are very regular looking. What makes them different than mosquitos in the lower 48 is that they are strong and resilient little buggers. Try to swat it, it will avoid you with ease. Smash it, it will do a pushup off the ground, spit in your face and tell you to try harder next time. This is of course an exaggeration, but honestly, they come in droves, it won't just be one mosquito, it will be forty. Strangely enough, we didn't use bug spray almost our entire trip. Talking to a local she basically advised that you just deal with them, and that bug spray doesn't work all that well to deter them anyways. So, we just dealt with it. Many places didn't have any mosquitos, some hikes were bad, but you just keep moving and they leave you alone. Some camp spots were horrible like this one, but you just get out of these areas as quickly as possible. Occasionally you'll see a big mosquito, almost three times bigger than usual with crazy long legs. We dubbed these the terrifying big brother of mosquitos. Funny enough, these are mosquito-eaters. They don't bite you they eat the guys trying to bite you. Scary as they look, leave them be.

# Soldotna

This is the last *big* town before the final push towards Homer. On your way here from Cooper Landing you'll notice the landscape change dramatically. From Anchorage all the way past Cooper Landing, the view is defined by the rolling hills, mountains, and breathtaking glaciers visible from the highway of the Chugach and Kenai Mountain ranges. Driving towards Soldotna, those horizon enhancing features fade away into a flat land of trees, tall grasses and shrubs. It's remarkable how quickly the scenery changes but when it does you know you're getting close to your next destination.

Soldotna is where you'll want to stock up on groceries and any other supplies because from here south prices will go up. We did find some very reasonably priced Oreos in Homer but that's for a later chapter. Here in Soldotna, we filled our fridge and our water tank and were gifted a jar of home cured salmon by a guy we offered to help in the water fill line at Fred Meyers. It never hurts to offer a hand.

We used quite a few of our coupons here for bagels and coffee. It's very common in Alaska (and in the Pacific Northwest in general) to have tiny shacks at the side of the road operating as delicious espresso stands. In Soldotna there are quite a few of these tiny-home coffee shops to choose from so skip the standard coffee chains and support a local brew. Speaking of brews there are tons of breweries all over Alaska. In almost every town you can find a local brewery including Kenai River Brewing and St Elias Brewing Company in Soldotna.

You're welcome to camp in the Fred Meyers parking lot, but we wanted something more scenic and opted for an ocean front spot twenty minutes outside of town. From here we had a gorgeous view of Lake Clark National Park and Preserve from an overhanging cliffside. There were a few other campers in this dirt lot, but everyone was quiet and respectful. It was very cool to watch the fishermen pulling in their nets along the coastline and the egrets and seagulls flying above.

After refitting in Soldotna, we had one more stop before Homer in Anchor Point. Another beach front free camping spot this time right on the water. We stayed at this spot twice as well, once on the way south and again on the way back north. The sunsets here are out of this world. On a clear day you can see a massive mountain range in the distance and all day every day the waves gently lapping at the shore are so peaceful. After a few days relaxing at the Alaskan beach, you'll be sun kissed and blissed out. Around 8pm, the fishermen return with their catch and a swarm of seagulls and eagles circle them hoping for some tossed aside guts, which the fishermen are happy to provide to keep the birds away from the good meat. It was like watching a National Geographic wildlife documentary.

# Homer and Seldovia

Homer is the furthest point south you can drive on the Kenai Peninsula, which is how it got its nickname *the end of the road*. It's also the halibut fishing capital of the world, according to who I don't know but they are very proud of that. You can charter many a boat to head out fishing for not only halibut, but salmon too (halibut gets the cheeky abbreviation of *butt* so if you see *bucket of butts* on the menu, you're ordering halibut). The Spit is the real attraction in Homer - a 4.5-mile stretch of land jutting out into Kachemak Bay. Lined with RV parking lots, beaches, fishing piers, fish gutting stations, public washrooms and townhome styled shops painted in bright colors, the Spit is *the* tourist destination of Homer and why so many people flock here.

There are tons of cute stores, coffee shops, pubs and restaurants to explore while you're here. We had an overpriced but decent meal at Harbor Bar and Grill and then decided to save our money and eat in, but we did hear great things about A Bus Named Sue and the Salty Dawg Saloon that's housed in a building older than Alaska itself.

We splurged on a few fancy coffees and a screen print for our wall art collection of a whale bopping a kayak but can see how it would be very easy to get sucked into spending a whole lot of dollars as you peruse from shop to shop.

We did a sightseeing tour out of the Homer harbor which is unique in and of itself as it had to be designed for a daily twenty-foot swell. The tour was very colorful as we were on a boat named the Rainbow Connection with Rainbow Tours. It was reasonably priced at about $70 per person for a seven-hour sightseeing cruise to the landlocked town of Seldovia. Along the way we saw otters, all kinds of birds and multiple packs of orca whales. The boat would stop from time to time to allow everyone to take photos and enjoy the wildlife before moving on.

When we got to Seldovia we had three hours to explore the once booming fishing village whose popularity plummeted when the road from Anchorage to Homer was completed in 1951. The village was stunning and quaint, known for its annual wood carving competitions.

There are wooden statues everywhere depicting everything from mermaids to giant mosquitos. As cute as the town is, I can understand why its residents chose to be a few hours' drive from civilization instead of a few hours' boat ride. When we were there the entire village was having a power outage that could only be fixed by having someone fly in from Anchorage to flip a switch. This must happen regularly as the local residents were completely unfazed.

On the Spit we spent one night in a campground as we weren't sure exactly where to park since all the other lots looked packed and had lots of complicated parking rule signs. We were with the Newstates who suggested the city run Fishing Hole Campground as the least expensive in the area at $20 per night. There are no hookups, but they do have a fee station dump and water fill. They do not accept reservation, so it's first come first serve. When we were there only half of the sixteen camp sites were full.

Then Drifter Journey let us in on their secret stealthy spot. They had booked an overnight boat cruise that dropped them off somewhere in Kachemak Bay State Park where they went for a big hike and tent camped before getting picked up the next morning and returned to civilization.

When asking the tour company where they should park their rig while out camping, they suggested the lot we've linked to in the coordinates section of this guide. They parked there the night before, the night of, and the night after their camping adventure without any issues, so we figured we would join them. As it turns out that is exactly what this lot is designed for so you're not breaking any rules by staying there. Our advice would be to stay stealthy about it though. We kept our window covers up and generally pretended we weren't home.

For showers on the Spit there are a few options including the Sportsman's Supply and RV and the Homer Spit Campground both at $7 each so we decided on the campground. These showers turned out to be lovely wood lined booths each with a dressing area before the actual shower. A bit tight but unlimited hot water was an amazing treat after a few days of dreary cold drizzle on the Spit.

If you're a self-proclaimed dirt bag like some friends of ours, you can take a bucket over to the concrete box of a public washroom and clean yourself up real nice. Make sure to find a stall that actually has hot water and you're golden.

I only tell you this because that's where friends of ours showered while we were there and although I think it is incredibly admirable of them to save the $14 for another day, I burst into an uncontrollable laughing fit when I used the toilets and imagined how unpleasant it would be to be any degree of naked in that stall. Maybe that means I'm not as hard core or full-fledged van lifer as they are. My standards are low, but they aren't quite that low… yet.

The mainland town of Homer has a good-sized grocery store where you can get some deals (like very cheap Oreo cookies – we bought three family sized boxes for like $5) but even residents here head to Soldotna for their big grocery shopping trips. We also found an incredibly well-priced spa, the Homer Inn and Spa, where we relaxed for three hours between their hot tub, sauna, and massage chair room all overlooking Kachemak Bay and the Aleutian Mountain Range. They have several different packages. We chose the most expensive (without a massage) for only $67 a person - well worth it. As we retraced our steps from Homer back to Anchorage our only regret was not visiting Hope. We heard from more than a few people that it's a lovely town nestled about 15 miles off the Seward highway on the other side of the Turnagain Arm - you can almost see it from Beluga Point.

The main attraction in Hope is a bar that has amazing live music every weekend. They also have several restaurants and hikes in the area that make it well worth a visit. Drifter Journey said it was their favorite place in all of Alaska, but we just never hit the timing right. Because the town is so small, it's only busy on the weekends and many of the restaurants and shops aren't open early in the week. Both on our way south and north we ended up traveling on a Monday or Tuesday, so it didn't make sense to head over there. Alas, we had to leave a few stones unturned for our next visit.

After exploring the Kenai Peninsula and making your way back towards Anchorage, you've still got a lot of Alaska to see. This was a strange transition for us as by now we'd been in the state for almost a month. It felt like we'd explored so much and at the same time as though we'd barely scratched the surface of all that Alaska had to offer. One local warned there wasn't much beauty in the north, not like in the Kenai. We beg to differ. Sure, it's different in its vastness and landscape., You're leaving behind the coastal towns (for the most part) and welcoming huge landscapes with mountain ranges boasting some of the tallest peaks in North America. There is a whole lot of beauty north of Anchorage so let's get ready to discover it.

# Palmer and Wasilla

After leaving Anchorage and visiting Eklutna, you'll arrive in the Palmer, Wasilla area. These are two towns of roughly the same size that seem to spill into each other. With their city centers only 11 miles apart, Wasilla is the larger of the two by population (10,000 to 7,000) and more than double the geographical size of Palmer as well (13 miles squared to 5).

Wasilla is another great place to grab groceries and other supplies. This is where we visited our first Three Bears, a chain of super stores akin to Costco. They even carry the Kirkland brand. Our favorite treat from Three Bears is Pure Organics Layered Fruit Bars. After eating our way through an entire box, we made a special trip back to Three Bears to buy two more boxes before leaving Alaska. We also got showers at the laundromat in town which was a solid okay for an on the road shower, just don't go over your time limit or you'll pay, literally.

Palmer felt like a much cooler town. We hung out at 203 Kombucha, a non-alcoholic brewery with a sweet food truck next door. Their picnic tables, food truck, and outdoor games made for a very fun afternoon. On the backside of the brewery building is Poppy Lane Mercantile, a super cute shop featuring all things Alaskan made. After getting tipsy on kombucha, I spent a pretty penny at Poppy Lane - it felt very orchestrated.

Then we headed north about 30 minutes of both cities towards Hatcher Pass which is technically in Willow. Here you can tour Independence Mine, an old gold mining operation that has since gone into ruin and is now designated as a national historical site. It's a neat place for an afternoon stroll learning about the history of the area from the interpretive signs. This site is dog friendly as are most places in Alaska.

It was incredibly easy to find dog friendly hikes and most stores and other establishments, even restaurants didn't care at all about us bringing Paco. In Alaska, dogs are a security system. If you're out on a hike and a wild animal comes up on you, you'll be glad you brought your four pawed friend.

Our furry friend is more of a risk than a security feature. He's so small he could get scooped up by an eagle or become an appetizer for a hungry coyote but big hearty working dogs, like most Alaskans choose, offer real protection.

Right next to Independence Mine is the entrance to Hatcher Pass. From about zero to 3,886 ft, this side of the pass is the sketchiest. It's much steeper and has more drastic switchbacks than the backside of the pass. At the top you have a few hikes to choose from including one that takes you all the way to the top of the mountain overlooking the entire area. Unfortunately, you can't sleep overnight at the top of Hatcher Pass so we continued on heading down the other side of the pass into a giant meadow.

The back side of the pass has much longer more drawn-out switch backs which makes for an easier ride. Funnily enough Google Maps shows this drive as a straight line which is very incorrect. We didn't have any issues traversing in either direction. Conditions were dry and we waited at Independence Mine, watching the cars and trucks going up the hill until we noticed traffic was dying down.

At the bottom of the backside of the hill, take your first right and decide how deep into the wilderness you want to negotiate. We weren't feeling all that adventurous so took the first spot which offered a great view of Hatcher Pass and the surrounding valley.

When we woke up the next morning the entire area had sunk into a cloud. There was zero visibility at the top of the pass (heck there was almost no visibility out our front window) so we waited until about noon for some of the fog to lift, but the clouds were so dense it felt like we would be waiting forever so decided to venture out. We did get some good sky and visibility when we got back to the top, but it didn't last long enough for us to hike to the peak.

Back in town, there are two places we didn't get a chance to visit but hope you will when you go. First up is I Dough Know, a drive-up food truck donut shop with a rotating flavor menu of out of this world combinations like raspberry chocolate chip, guava passion fruit, chocolate caramel pecan, and of course champagne. Get there early because they sell out quickly and check which days, they are open. Sadly, we never quite made it in time.

The second attraction we are saving for next time is the Alaska State Fair. It runs from late August to early September and hosts all kinds of entertainment from musical acts to carnival rides and of course all the food your state fair dreams are made of. The best food trucks from all over the state pack up and head to Palmer for their last week of business of the season at the fair. Find the spinach bread truck for us too please.

We only slept in Palmer one night and then opted for a location about twenty minutes outside of town. In town we used the iOverlander spot called Matanuska River which was nice and the guy who lives here permanently in his broken-down yellow box truck was very friendly if not a little bit drunk. It sounds like you can park right downtown, but we prefer more wild places so headed just outside of town where friends shared their favorite iOverlander spot with us called Kings River. Here we had excellent connectivity so we could work while still being close enough to town to drive in and check on our broken-down laptop at Rent-a-Geek. We ended up having the most amazing experience just because we were parked there.

This spot always has a few different campers at it, so we nestled ourselves away from the crowd in the nook where the Kings and Matanuska rivers collide, one so blue it looked like teal, the other slate grey from kicked up glacier rocks that had been disturbed by recent rains. After eating dinner on our front porch (a rolled out weatherproof mat with two camping chairs) we went in for the night. For some reason, maybe tantalized by the beautiful mountain views surrounding us, Frankie stepped outside just as an older gentleman was ridding by on his four-wheeler. After a lengthy conversation covering all topics from Icelandic relatives (his) to decades of career choices, Frankie asked our new friend Kevin where we might go for a nice hike in the area. Kevin advised he didn't know much about hikes, but that he had two more four-wheelers and would be happy to gas them up and take us on an adventure the next day.

We gladly accepted and as promised, first thing the next morning Kevin picked us up in his pristine vintage truck and we were off. What ensued was a full day of intense four-wheeling in some of Alaska's most wild places. We climbed rocks, road over giant tree roots and through knee deep puddles all while steadily climbing up, and up, and up to the Alaskan tundra. Our reward for seven hours of hard labor, turns out riding a four-wheeler is physically exhausting, was a magical view we would have never experienced otherwise. Paco rode along in Frankie's backpack the whole day and I did my best not to kill anyone, mainly myself, as I kept crashing into things and flipping the dang ATV.

It was a memorable experience to say the least. We spent the next two nights camped in Kevin's driveway, cooking him dinner, swapping stories and nursing my many aches and bruises. We won't be sharing Kevin's information in this guide but if you happen to see an incredibly handsome, could be a hair model, dignified older gentleman riding by on his four-wheeler, tell him Frankie and Alex sent you.

# Glacier View and Glennallen

After saying goodbye to Kevin, we picked up the Glenn Highway driving eastward towards Glennallen. We had a few very special stops along the way worth mentioning here. The first was a spot our friends Fenimore's Adventure More and Out of This Van invited us to. I'm not sure if this is just in the van life community but we tend to call each other by our Instagram names not our real names, especially when it's a couple.

Out of This Van took the ferry from Bellingham, but with the direct transit to Whittier sold out, they fenagled an alternate route. It's recommended to book the ferry in January when the summer schedule is released but Evan and Melanny only booked it three weeks before they left. This didn't leave a lot of options because the direct route by this time was sold out. They departed Bellingham for Ketchikan and spent two weeks exploring there before catching another open spot on the boat to Juneau.

They planned on staying there for a month but got on the same day waitlist for an earlier boat and were boarded on the Kennicott ship heading for Whittier just two weeks after arrival.

Their lucky streak continued oddly enough with a boat breakdown, the bonus of which was that the ferry company dropped them off in Haines allowing them to do a stretch of the ALCAN highway through Canada and they got a big chunk of cash refunded since they didn't make it all the way to Whittier. Even though it was a little bit messy and I'm sure stressful trying to figure everything out, Out of This Van loved their cruise on the inside passage, something people pay mega bucks for. They also tent camped in the solarium of the boat which they said was an amazing experience. Our other friends Travels with Kevan got the state rooms and complained they were loud and creaky and warned not to expect a good night's sleep especially considering how much they cost.

The Fenimore's drove up through Canada with work papers from their company (something that likely won't be needed next year as Canada is already open to fully vaccinated travelers) and the two couples met by chance on a hike in Wrangell St Elias National Park, just east of Glennallen. They were on their way west and we were on our way east, so we met in the middle for a few days of relaxation and connection in Glacier View.

Wrangell St Elias National Park and Preserve is another place we still want to visit. This time around it didn't make the cut because we were operating on a time crunch, our days in Alaska getting shorter and shorter. We chose to forgo a visit to Wrangell based on time and talks with Fenimore and Out of This Van. They thoroughly enjoyed the park and went on some amazing hikes but noted that the park is hard to get to, many miles on dirt roads, and beyond a few hikes, there's not much else to do.

There are two roads into the park. The Nabesna Road to the north is a gravel road that is 42 miles long with three stream crossings. The McCarthy Road is the more traveled route accessed via the south jutting off from the highway towards Valdez. It is also gravel and 59 miles long but there are no river crossings. There are many pull offs along the road to sleep for a few nights as you make your way into and out of the park but be warned there is no fuel, so you'll want to fill your tank before you go and make sure you have enough gas to get back out. From the sounds of it the road is manageable though long and bumpy, so we opted for a different long and bumpy road instead, the Denali highway, but we'll chat about that later.

For now, we spent three nights hanging out by a rushing river at a spot on iOverlander aptly listed as *Down by the River* in Glacier View. I never looked at the listing until now because our friends sent us the coordinates to meet them, but I find it kind of hilarious the original poster mentions a possibly unreliable bridge because we helped rebuild that bridge. Let me explain.

During our first full day at the spot, we were enjoying the sunshine, sitting around in our camp chairs, swapping stories and playing with the dogs (each couple has their own). In the afternoon, several folks started working on the bridge. We didn't pay them too much attention as the bridge is long and they started on the other side but by the time they worked their way over to us, we were intrigued by what they were doing. That question was answered almost right away when one of the members of the group rolled up on us driving his four-wheeler with a pull-behind blue trailer.

At first, I must admit I was worried he was coming to run us out of town, but Jim was excited to chat. He wanted to learn where we came from, where we were going and of course he wanted to share many stories about his wild and well-traveled life. Jim invited us to come over to his place, on the other side of the bridge later that evening and we gladly accepted.

The community on the land on the other side of the bridge was all originally owned by one man. Over the years he sold off 5-acre parcels to his friends and folks he trusted. He created a community of people who will all pull up their bootstraps to help each other, help the collective and help fix the only bridge into or out of their island. The following day work recommenced, and Frankie joined the crew laying new beams of wood atop the metal bridge. Many hands make light work and so the job only took a few hours. We were happy to charge power tools with our outlets and they rewarded Frankie with sugar cookies. After chatting with them for a few hours more, they returned home, and we returned to our vans for the night.

The next day our van crew decided it was time to leave this wonderful spot but before we parted ways, we decided to do the hardest hike we've ever attempted. Gunsight Mountain is a 3.7-mile hike straight up the side of a mountain. The start of the hike is well traveled by ATVs but the higher you get, even the machines give up and it's impossible to know if you're on trail except for the fact you can see the peak in the distance and you're generally heading that way.

We started around 11am and didn't get back to the vans until around 5pm, tired, soar, sun burnt and covered in mud from an unfortunate slip into a giant puddle. All that aside, the views at the top were spectacular. I personally would have enjoyed the views better from a helicopter, but with that clearly not in our budget, we took the two-foot express.

The main attraction in Glacier View is the Matanuska Glacier. This 27mile long 4-mile-wide glacier is one of the most accessible technically, but you have to buy a tour to walk on it. There used to be a self-guided trail marked off by cones that you could wander by yourself. Because the glacier has become more unstable in the last number of years, the only way you're allowed to access it now is with a tour guide. The benefit of this is that they set you up with all the equipment to safely climb all over the glaciers. Both Fenimore and Out of This Van enjoyed their guided tours, but we opted not to spend the $300.

You might be noticing a theme that by the second half of our journey, we were feeling the budget crunch. Getting to Alaska was expensive; being in the hotel waiting for our van was expensive; eating out in Alaskan restaurants was expensive. We splurged for the jet ski tour, the boat cruise, and the spa. With all that plus the coffees and groceries and restaurant meals in between our credit card was getting a workout. We knew that the summer in Alaska was going to eat into our pocket and that's okay, but we wanted to make sure we were making the best choices with our cash. Since neither of us were feeling incredibly drawn to this specific tour, we took a pass.

Don't forget to visit Old Bear Honey on your way out of town for some delicious Alaskan treats, local grown veggies and honey of all kinds. It's run by the son of the original owner of the island whose bridge we helped repair, so we would be incredibly grateful for you to pop in there for a visit because they are lovely folks.

The last stop in this chapter is Glennallen. This small town Ts off the Glenn and Richardson highways. As you drive toward Glennallen the mountain range in front of you looks insanely large - it dominates the entire horizon. From this vantage point, you are looking at the western most mountains in the Wrangell St Elias Mountain range. The grocery store in town is very expensive but the post office was nice, and we had some tasty fish and chips at a gas station restaurant. We found an amazing spot to camp with a stunning view of a forest and mountains atop a 100-foot cliff with no guardrails. We stayed here twice, once on our way south and again as we traveled north. I would not recommend this spot if you don't like heights or if your emergency break doesn't work. We weren't all that close to the cliff, but it felt good to throw on the e-break just in case. After a peaceful night's sleep on the edge of a death-defying cliff, we headed south and found one of the most beautiful drives in all of Alaska.

# Valdez

We thought we'd seen all the amazing beauty Alaska had to offer, but when we left Glennallen for Valdez, we were blown away all over again. As the Richardson highway continues south, you drive through mountains, glaciers, and more waterfalls that you can possibly take in in just one drive. Luckily you have to retrace your steps to get out of Valdez which means you get to do the drive at least twice. On our way in we had stunning weather and could see breathtaking beauty all around for miles.

The pinnacle of the drive is at the top of Thompson Pass, a 2,678-foot-high mountain pass through the Chugach Mountains and the snowiest place in Alaska with over 500 inches of snow on average per year. When we were there in early August there was no snow to be found but the views were insane. It was a bit windy, but we were able to get the drone up and capture some spectacular views. On the way out of Valdez, it was rainy and overcast and we couldn't see anything at all. So please, please, please, do the pass on a clear day. It will be worth the wait.

The port town of Valdez has in interesting history. After the massive Good Friday earthquake, the residents of the town realized they were on unstable ground. The original site of the town was deemed unfit for habitation, so they relocated the entire town three miles down the road. Although not all the locals were happy about it at the time, it gave them the opportunity to completely rethink and redesign how the town was laid out. You can take a tour of the old town, which is basically a tall grass field, but there are interpretive signs and photographs where the old buildings once stood. We did this on our ebike ride through town and thought it was cool to see this slice of history. If you're a real history buff you'll want to visit the Valdez Museum where you can learn all about the relocation as well as the 1989 oil spill that put Valdez on the front of every newspaper (some of the locals we met swear the whole thing is a conspiracy and that there's no way the boat should have crashed, but that's all hearsay).

During our stay in Valdez, we camped at Robe Lake and also on a very cool peninsula. There were tons of spots listed on iOverlander that are all technically on the outskirts of town, but *town* isn't that big and the drive to get anywhere from these supposedly *remote* sites is only about ten minutes. Also on the outskirts of town is The Solomon Gulch Hatchery where if you time it right, you can see the salmon returning home to spawn. We were told this happens in mid-August but the best way to find out is to call a local fishing charter and ask if they are seeing any action yet.

For me this was kind of hard to watch since they are literally returning home to be gutted for their eggs and sperm then turned into dog food. But after talking with our supermodel friend Kevin, we felt much better about it. Kevin has a stream in his front yard where salmon naturally return to spawn every year. After they do their baby-making business, they die from the exertion of the trip. Their corpses rot and freeze over the winter only to become food for the new babies in the Spring.

The hatchery is really just flowing with the cycle of life, except the moms and dads are eaten by cats and dogs instead of their babies who are well fed at the hatchery and returned to sea for their two-to-three-year lifespan. At the hatchery there's always a chance of seeing sea lions or bears feasting on the thousands of fish swimming upstream. Sea lions are common, we saw many of them feeding, but bears are hard to spot. The only bear we saw in Valdez was a grizzly running along the side of the main road into town alongside our van - that was cool. At the hatchery, they prefer to feed at dusk or dawn.

Downtown Valdez itself is incredibly cute. It's a harbor town so there's lots of boat and harbor activity to watch. We were told you can stealth camp right in the harbor for a few nights but didn't investigate because after being parked there for an hour with some crazy tools making horrible noises in the background, we needed to get as far away from there as possible. There are a few delicious restaurants to try in town.

The Thai food truck Aunty Yum Yum's served up full plate sized authentic Thai food at just under $20 a pop. The Potato was our real favorite cause their spuds were fantastic and prices more moderate. Shoestring cut and covered in fresh garlic and fresh herbs; they were honestly the best fries I've ever had. We also grabbed two vegan wraps and if you're into it they have many different beer options to choose from. The vibe here is friendly and local with everyone sharing picnic tables overlooking the harbor.

The two biggest restaurants in town were closed when we were there. The Fat Mermaid is at the top of every internet list for places to eat in Valdez with Nat Shack coming in at a close second. The owner of Nat Shack died unexpectedly right before we got there. It was a big loss for the whole community as he was a pillar of their town and all the kind words written about him online make us disappointed, we never got to meet him. The Fat Mermaid was open the first day we arrived, but the patio was packed, and we heard there was a long wait, so we took a pass. The next day and the rest of the time we were there it was closed and as there was a help wanted sign on the door, we can only speculate it had staffing issues.

We did one big hike in Valdez but there are plenty to choose from as well as a 6.5-mile-long waterfront trail to walk, run, ride or rollerblade on. The hike we did was called Solomon Lake Trail, past the hatchery and about one mile beyond where the internet says the trailhead is. After walking five miles mainly uphill on a hot day we were excited to jump into any body of water. The lake by the dam didn't look as welcoming as the small swimming hole we passed on the way up, so we headed back down and took a dip in the crystal-clear waters heated by dark stones absorbing the sun.

For summer activities in Valdez, kayaking is the thing to do. There are a few companies in town that will take you out on guided excursions ranging from half-day to overnight trips visiting all kinds of wildlife and glaciers along the way. We opted to take a self-guided kayak tour with Valdez Stay and Play for a third of the price. Glacier Lake is named for the Valdez glacier that is melting into it and dropping massive icebergs along the way. The water is frigid and bottoms out at over 600 feet deep.

After a quick instructional from the owner of Valdez Stay and Play which included such tips as "if there are bubbles around the icebergs get away from it because it's about to flip" and of course "don't walk on the icebergs, they are very unstable" we were off! The icebergs are like giant floating puzzle pieces forming a maze to get to the glacier. If reaching the glacier is your ultimate goal, definitely hire a guide to take you there because every single day the route to get to it changes. If your goal is to have a rip-roaring good time goofing off in potentially dangerous waters, take the self-guided tour. Frankie and I had so much fun becoming self-proclaimed *berg hunters* that our three hours on the water went by in a flash.

We enjoyed ourselves so much that the next day we decided to do another tour with Valdez Stay and Play. This time they sent us out on their very nice e-bikes with a map of Valdez and a suggested route. This took us from the old Valdez town site to Mineral Creek with stunning waterfalls (our friends Adaptive Humanity camped out beyond these falls and loved it; you do have to cross at least one creek).

We had a great time exploring Valdez by ebike carting Paco in a little dog carrier (also rented) behind us. It was very nice to be out exploring on our own. Tours are great and all but sometimes you just want to be on your own schedule having your own fun.

For showers we went to the iOverlander recommended harbor and they were horrible. Not hot enough with cold air blowing through the dingy concrete bathroom the whole time. We found out literally an hour later when we were looking for somewhere to do laundry that there is a new harbor with super fancy showers for the exact same price five minutes away. I was pissed having just paid for a horrible shower but got to experience the good ones before we left town and oh man were they a hundred thousand times better. We updated the iOverlander listing because no one should have to go through that ever again.

Valdez is one of those places often missed on people's tours in Alaska, probably because it's a bit out of the way from the headliners of Kenai and Denali. I would highly suggest you add it to your list because it was one of our favorite spots in all of Alaska and one of those places that takes a place in your heart forever.

# Talkeetna

If we had looked at a map before choosing Talkeetna as our next stop, I don't think we would have gone. We heard from multiple people that Talkeetna is the best place to see Denali, the jumping off point for all Denali excursions, and yes both those statements are true. But it's also 154 miles south of the Denali National Park entrance and we were coming from the north, whoopsie. In any case I'm very glad we went out of our way to go there because it's such a cool town.

Talkeetna is a little bit of a tourist trap, with one main strip of shops and businesses making up the majority of what you'll be exploring while you're there. The entire place gives off such cool hippy vibes that it's just nice to wander around. You can grab a cup of coffee from a building with a giant happy face painted on the roof or pick up handcrafted salves and tinctures from Alaskan grown medicinal plants.

We had a tasty pizza and took a cheesy photo with pizza wings at Mountain High Pizza Pie, which also has live music and a popping bar. You can buy hand forged Alaskan knifes or birch bark baskets at a local made market and there are plenty of food trucks and restaurants to satisfy any appetite. After exploring the main strip, take a walk by the waterfront to chill out and if you're lucky, see Denali.

There is a small tent campground near the water that you could maybe get into if you're in a true van life van. We did see some bigger rigs parked down there on the street with placards on them from the campground so they must have an agreement with the city. We chose to camp in a parking spot right around the main park in town. There was a guy living out of his blue sedan who had clearly been there for quite some time, and we saw no "no parking" signs so figured it would be a good place to crash for a night. We ended up staying three nights and were joined by a number of other van-sized rigs while we were there. For your park side location try to get as far away from the Fairview Inn as possible as the bar gets loud even on random weeknights.

You can sign up for lots of tours of Denali from here including flights or dog sleds, but we just enjoyed the sights, foods, and vibes of this kitschy little town before embarking on our own adventure to Denali National Park.

# Denali National Park

Denali Mountain is the highest peak in North America at 20,310-feet and is the crowing jewel of the Alaska Range. To our surprise, Denali National Park isn't the best place to see the mountain from. You can see it from many different places in Anchorage including the waterfront, the top of Flattop Mountain and even from the top of the JC Penney parking garage. Talkeetna is the next best place with multiple viewing locations in town and just outside of it. Heck you can even see it from Fairbanks it's so big.

On the Parks Highway (still technically outside the park) you've got both Denali Viewpoint North and Denali Viewpoint South in Trapper Creek. There are campgrounds at both locations that have stunning views of Denali. The joke about Denali is that most people who come here, never see it. The mountain is covered in clouds seven out of ten days so it's lucky if you do get to see it from any of these viewpoints.

Inside the National Park, you can't see Denali from the campgrounds. You'll have to get yourself on a bus to experience the parks namesake. Let me backtrack a little bit to set the scene of what it's like to camp inside Denali (and kick myself for not having done this research before we got there, thankfully I'm doing the legwork for you now). To book a campsite in Denali is a headache and a half. You must book it via their website which isn't the easiest to navigate. There are a few campgrounds in the park but everyone and their mother told us we simply had to book Teklanika River Campground. It is the furthest in campground you can drive to at mile 29. There are two additional campgrounds way deep in the park at mile 85 but you have to take a bus to these and tent camp. For Teklanika, also known as Tek, there is a three-night minimum. If one of the three nights you request is booked online, they will tell you there is no availability, so adjust your search until you find three available days in a row.

We booked about two weeks ahead and didn't have much trouble booking the campground – although we were later informed that we booked it wrong and owed double what we paid because somehow, we booked a senior's rate which apparently happens all the time. Again, the website is trash. The trouble came when we went to book the bus. Once you are at the Tek campground you are not allowed to drive your car again until you're leaving the park. That means the only way to explore the remaining sixty miles of the park road is by bus or bicycle. If I were to do it again, if possible, I would bring an electric bike with me to explore the park because this would be the best way to experience Denali in my opinion.

The buses were completely sold out, so we took our chances and waited until 48 hours before we checked in, woke up at the crack of dawn and called the National Park to try and book one of their last-minute bus passes. We got two passes at about $60 each for the basic Tek pass which is apparently the same as a transit pass even though everyone and their mother said you must get a Tek pass. Everyone and their mother were wrong about a lot of Denali.

When we arrived at the visitor center, we were excited and ready for this next adventure. Our dreams were quickly dashed by the lack of enthusiasm at the check in desk. The two folks checking us in where the grumpiest National Parks employees I've ever encountered. First, they informed us we owned double what we paid, then they talked smack about whoever was just on the phone for not being able to book their campground properly, then they went through a list of about a hundred rules for camping in the park. I get that these rules are important, and we followed them to a T, but their delivery was so blasé and condescending it was almost laughable.

As you drive to your campground, you're allowed to stop wherever you like, take photos, go for a hike or just smell the flowers, just keep moving in one direction because you're not allowed to drive back. If we were to do this again, we would have stopped and taken ourselves for a hike but not knowing the lay of the land at all, we didn't feel comfortable doing this.

The campground itself was nice enough. Each spot had a fire ring and picnic table, and they were nicely separated by foliage so not right on top of each other. There are two loops of sites and we tried to position ourselves as close to the river as possible which meant our backyard was glorious. Because of all the rules about dogs we could only explore the main roads with Paco so that limited our walks from camp. Each campground loop has a pit toilet bathroom and water spicket for filling buckets or doing dishes, not filling your camper tank. There's a spot for that near the entrance to the park so fill up before you head to camp.

Perhaps it was a symptom of the year we came, but honestly it didn't seem like it was worth all the fuss. Sure, we didn't have any trouble booking the site which can be hard in other years. The bus pass was cheaper than a tour company, but maybe the tour company wouldn't have rushed us through every stop and threatened to leave without us if we weren't on the bus in 5… 4… 3…. It was like being wrangled for a class trip in elementary school.

The buses were about the same quality as your school day memories and despite all their talk about social distancing and pandemic precautions, we were crammed in without a single empty seat (the expensive buses looked equally packed). Then when the wildlife came by, we were encouraged to crawl over our neighbors to look out their windows. But heaven forbid if you take your mask off for a moment or forget to put it back on when you're entering the bus. Hell hath no fury like a bus driver enforcing a mask mandate. Maybe it was our particular bus driver, but by the end of the very long eight-hour day on the bus, I had a splitting headache and Frankie was completely exhausted.

I hate to complain and certainly don't want to color your Denali experience with our somewhat crummy time. Maybe it's a good thing we are setting the bar low for you so when you do get there you'll think, gosh this isn't at all as bad as FnA said it was. We went into it with an incredibly high expectations from what everyone saying, "Denali is the best thing to do in Alaska, you simply can't miss it!" and were sadly let down.

If we were to do it again, I think we would still stay at Tek but instead of trying to get all the way to the Eielson Visitor Center on the bus like we were recommended to do, I would get off somewhere along the highway and go for one of the famed backcountry hikes. Denali used to have ranger led backcountry hikes but those were put on hold when the pandemic hit. If those came back, I would sign up in a heartbeat as we heard they were amazing. Perhaps we should count ourselves lucky that we got to go all the way in because the road into Denali has since been cut off due to erosion. When we were there, we spoke with some of the folks trying to fix one particular section of the road by dumping over 100 trucks of gravel into it that year alone and it was still crumbling away. As of this writing, the bus isn't going past mile 42 so be sure to check on it before you book.

Just outside of the park, heading north on the Parks Highway, is a row of shops and restaurants designed to service all the visitors to the park. We stopped here for the best pizza we had in all of Alaska at Prospectors Pizza. Then slightly north of that in Healy, we grabbed a decent shower at Tri-Valley Gas and continued our adventures towards the biggest town in the north.

# Fairbanks

The largest city in the Interior, nearly half of Fairbanks' population is made up of military personal because of the nearby air force base. You can see and hear jets planes flying above at all times of day. Fairbanks is also known for being very hot in the summer and very cold in the winter. Up here it's all about extremes with temperatures dropping below -25 F in the winter and getting all the way up to 99 F in the summer.

Fairbanks is also famed for northern lights aurora viewing. If this is on your bucket list, you'll need to stick around until at least September to see them. When we left at the end of August, the season was just starting. You need the perfect combination of darkness and clear skies to be able to see them. We stayed up past 3am on our last day in the north trying to spot them but it was still dusk, and the clouds had taken over the sky by the time we crashed.

We drove to Fairbanks from Denali on the Parks Highway which was a nice albeit sparse drive. There's not much to see unless you want to stop for a beer or a night at Skinny Dick's Halfway Inn. There's also a giant manmade igloo that used to be a tourist attraction but has since shut down. It might be cool for a photo if you're into derelict building photography.

On the east, you can drive up from Glennallen through Delta Junction and hit the towns of North Pole and Delta Junction. If you're driving out of the state from Fairbanks, we recommend you take the eastern Steese Highway out through Tok. If you take the Northern route from here, you can visit the giant chicken statue in Chicken and ride along the Top of the World Highway. If you take the more common route through Beaver Creek, you get to drive along the Kluane National Park and Preserve in the Yukon.

Fairbanks is another great town to restock on supplies since you can find every kind of big box store here. What Fairbanks is lacking are places to boondock, especially in the city. You could probably park in one of those big box parking lots but if you want something more scenic, you're going to have to get out of town. We stayed one night at a highway overpass just south of the city on the Steese Highway which had a lovely view and was protected from the highway noise with a huge growth of trees. Our friends booked one night at the only Harvest Host in town. Boondockers Welcome also works in Alaska but we didn't see all that many options on the site for the whole state so eventually stopped looking up places to stay on it (the two companies are merging so you'll only need Harvest Host to access both from now on).

The rest of our time in Fairbanks we stayed in the parking lot of a hostel. Our friends worked there all summer at the front desk and so when we were coming to town we wanted to pop in and visit with them. The owner of Sven's Basecamp Hostel, Sven, invited us to stay in his parking lot after a long chat and a tour of our van. He welcomed us to stay at the hostel anytime we liked so we took advantage of his generosity a few times while we were in town. Having never stayed at a hostel before I really enjoyed the energy. There is a big communal table outside the kitchen where we sat for many hours chatting with the various guests who flowed into and out of the common area throughout the evening. It was lovely to hear all their stories, get ideas about where to visit, learn where they came from and how they ended up in Alaska. Sven's also has bathrooms and coin operated showers as well as bear spray rentals, a slack line, puppies to cuddle, a small community garden and so much more. I'm sure if you popped by and chatted with the front desk, you could work out how to camp in their parking lot for a night too.

The main attractions in Fairbanks are the Museum of the North, Georgeson Botanical Garden, the Moose Antler Arch and the Fairbanks Ice Museum of which we did none. When we got to Fairbanks, we met up with our friends Adaptive Humanity and spent our time reconnecting with them over some delicious Thai food. Fairbanks is known for having more Thai restaurants per capita than any other US city so we had to indulge. Our hostel friends said that Lemongrass Thai Restaurant is the best in town, and despite begin tucked away behind a gas station in a less than gorgeous strip mall, the food was excellent. Just don't make the same mistake Amber did by asking for it hot and then add all the chilies to it before tasting it - she was on fire.

If Thai isn't your jam, we were also recommended to visit Pita Place but unfortunately it was closed for the season by the end of August. It felt like a lot of businesses start to close shop by mid to late August as the weather turns cooler and the days start to get shorter. Many of the food trucks also relocate to the Alaska State Fair, so you can only visit them if you're taking a trip to Palmer in late August/early September.

After a wonderful reunion dinner, we spent the next day doing laundry and errands getting ready for our next adventure. For as big as Fairbanks looks on the map, it's actually a small town. To go from one side of downtown to the other is half a mile and pretty much everything there is to see and do in Fairbanks's proper is within that radius. One small offshoot and a lovely hike through aspens is Ester Dome (you can also camp up there but the iOverlander spot had a bunch of private property signs on it, so we didn't think we should). The hike however was lovely and operates as a sweet bike track with an inner and outer loop. The real attraction of Ester Dome is the local man who takes an 8 mile walk every day with his dog to get his mail. He is a character and a half and if you get him talking, good luck getting him to stop. Frankie was soaking it all up as they chatted baseball and the man ragged on Frankie for being from New York.

The more we travel the less we enjoy big cities. Fairbanks for us is a launching pad for adventures in parts unknown. We did spend a few days here on either end of our journey to the North. It was nice to see friends and eat some delicious Thai food, but the next chapter of our adventure was much more noteworthy.

# Up North of 60

Beyond Fairbanks is 500 miles of varying levels of questionable roads. The Dalton Highway is one of those travel check boxes that many folks are seeking to tik off. At the end of the road is Prudhoe Bay also known as Dead Horse, the most northern part of the Pan-American Highway that goes all the way to Ushuaia, Argentina. Along the way you'll be surrounded by some of the most vast and uninhabited landscapes you'll ever see. Most of the traffic up here is related to the oil industry which is evident from the pipeline that runs alongside the highway for many miles.

At one point we noticed a fairly run-down wooden house surrounded by various broken-down cars almost directly under the pipeline. Thinking it was abandoned we stared intently as we drove by only to be greeted by an elderly woman walking out onto her front porch in her dressing gown just taking in the day. This was one of the only homes we saw along our way to the Arctic Circle.

We caravanned up here with Adaptive Humanity and are glad we had a buddy system. The further north we got, the less traffic we saw in either direction. It's not so remote that if you were broken down, you'd be alone for days but it's possible that hours could go by without seeing another living soul. It's recommended that if you are taking this adventure, you be self-sufficient and have tools, fluids, a spare tire and other safety measures to make sure if something were to happen you would be comfortable and safe; especially if you're making this drive in the fall or winter and are risking hypothermia if your engine dies.

We easily made it to the Arctic Circle in two days of moderate driving. We slept once at a large pull-off on the side of the Steese Highway just before it turned into the Dalton Highway and once at the Arctic Circle which has a large brand-new campground complete with fire rings and pit toilets. When we camped there in August of 2021, it was clear the place had just been finished and there were no signs about pricing. There might be a fee moving forward but because it's on BLM I can't imagine the cost would be prohibitive.

The prohibitive cost of this journey is the price of fuel. Fill up in Fairbanks before you leave but you'll need a few more tanks if you plan on making it all the way to Prudhoe and back. Fuel stations are few and far between, so it's worth stopping in and topping off your tank whenever you have the opportunity. You'll also probably be glad for a few moments to stretch your legs after another long stretch of bumpy road. We paid $5.50 a gallon to fuel up near the Yukon River and needed two tanks for our trip to and from form the Arctic Circle Sign. There's also little to no food options, especially if you enjoy fresh fruits and vegetables, so stock up on those before you leave as well.

We had no issues with our 2-wheel drive van as long as we remained vigilant during particularly bad sections where Frankie was dodging potholes left right and center. Otherwise, the road was fine, if not long bumpy, loud and boring. There's zero internet and not even a radio station so you'll want to stock up on audio books or music to keep yourself entertained for the long drive. Alternately, get a HAM radio and chat with the truckers on the road.

The reason we didn't continue further from the Arctic Circle Sign was purely because of a time constraint. As we delayed the drive waiting for Matt and Amber to arrive and with our deadline to leave Alaska inching closer every day, we didn't think it prudent to continue north knowing how long it was going to take to get back to Anchorage and catch our boat south. Beyond the Arctic Circle, is the Brooks Range. A man we met at Sven's advised this was the best spot on the entire Dalton Highway and if you're going to go all the way to the Arctic Circle Sign, you may as well continue another 158 miles for the best view on the entire highway at Galbraith Lake. Here you'll find another amazing free campground surrounded by stunning snowcapped mountains as far as the eye can see. As they continued their way north, Adaptive Humanity sent us multiple images of wild landscapes and even polar bears. The caveat of the Dalton is that it doesn't actually take you all the way to the Arctic Ocean. Prudhoe Bay is private property so if you want to dip your toe into the ocean, you'll need to pay for a bus to get there. It's $67 per person and takes you on a 1.5-hour bus ride complete with towels in case anyone wants to jump in and risk hypothermia.

Matt and Amber also learned that if you want to visit any of the remote towns up there, the most affordable place to do it from isn't right next door, it's all the way back in Fairbanks. It's much cheaper to charter flights to places like Kaktovik, Utqiagvik or Barrow from the biggest city in the north than from Prudhoe. Matt and Amber enjoyed their time up in the very remote north even trying local delicacies like whale (they also said there wasn't much else to eat in terms of fresh fruits and vegetables).

The other stop outside of Fairbanks you'll hear a lot about is Chena Hot Springs. This is one of the very few accessible hot springs in Alaska. Many require a long arduous hike, plane or boat ride to enjoy them, but Chena is right at the end of Chena Hot Spring Road only 60 miles from Fairbanks. This area has been built up over the years to house many a tourist attraction. You can visit their giant ice museum, open year-round filled with ice sculptures and even an artist in residence making martini glasses out of ice right in front of you. Be aware, the martinis are strong and there is a tradition to take the ice glass outside, make a wish and smash it on the floor.

The funny thing about Chena is that it's very much a veneer. The hot springs look lovely but don't touch the floor because the faux gravel is caked in hair and other debris. The locker rooms are huge but in a state of wetness 100% of the time and the showers made us feel dirtier than the pools. The ice museum was neat but the jackets they offer you to wear (and you're going to want to wear a coat, it is beyond cold in there) are sprayed down with disinfectant so when you put one on, you'll be inhaling the fumes of antibacterial spray your whole tour which was only about thirty minutes and $60 per person. It was cool but not so cool that I would be rushing back anytime soon. Oh, and you can't sleep there unless you want to pay to camp so we drove about fifteen minutes outside the resort and found a nice state-run roadside pull off that was an honor system payment of $5.

The best thing that happened at Chena was that we met a woman in the hot tub who invited us back to her place to give us a jar of homemade wild blueberry jam and a fresh jar of hand-picked blueberry juice she had just finished making. She also used to run an Airbnb where she would help tourists take photos of the aurora borealis. After an hour chatting with her, we learnt all about the best time of year to see them (basically all winter), the only locations you can see them from (the kp band that stretches around the earth), solar winds (the lights are basically a sun fart) and so much more. If we'd had more time we would have definitely stuck around her place for a night or two and got some photos of the northern lights with her, but at the least the jam was delicious.

Folks might be right that the north doesn't have the same sheen to it as the south does, but there is still so much to see and do here that it's well worth the visit. This was one of the only places in Alaska where we really felt like we were out there, deep in the wild. Even when you go off-grid in the south you know you're only a quick drive to the nearest town. In the north, you are truly in the Alaskan wilderness.

# Once in a Lifetime Adventure You Have to do Again

With all the logistics, time, miles and money it takes to get to Alaska, many people call it a once in a lifetime adventure. And I'm sure that's true for some, but for others, it's a once in a lifetime trip that results in a life-long love affair with the state. For us, we don't know when we'll be back, but we know we want to make it happen eventually. It was a bittersweet feeling leaving the 49$^{th}$ state. On one hand we felt lucky that we got to explore for the whole summer. We got to visit almost every town, skinny-dipped in freezing cold lakes, camped at the top of a cliffside, hung out with locals, ate so much good food and explored so much of the state. Most people only get a week or so to try and jam it all in. Van life offered us the luxury of time, to move as quickly or slowly as we liked.

When we got back to Washington, we both felt a pang of sadness and regret for having left Alaska. It's that phenomenon of post vacation blues where you're back to the regular world and you don't want to be.

We wondered what we missed, which stones we had left unturned, which adventures we had skipped over or didn't even know about. Yes, winter months were looming but, maybe that would be an exciting adventure as well. Maybe we could figure out how to make it work, maybe the cold wouldn't bother us so much. We had fallen in love so deeply that we actually contemplated cancelling all our plans to stay the winter in Alaska. Perhaps we could buy land somewhere or a local would take us in and we could boondock on their property. That's how much she draws you in. Alaska makes you seriously contemplate living months on end in frigid cold temperatures with only three to five hours of dusk like sun a day by offering you a summer of glorious views, a land bursting with life and beauty at every turn.

Will we be back? One hundred percent yes. When will that be? We have absolutely no idea. But one thing is for certain, Alaska will always hold a special place in our hearts.

# Coordinates for Where we Slept

During our time in Alaska, we started a series on Tik Tok chronicling where we slept the night before. This has since become one of our favorite things to share because it highlights how accessible and safe free camping is. When we first got on the road, finding safe places to sleep was one of our biggest concerns. Now that we've been on the road almost 2 years, it has become second nature. We don't even think or worry about our next stop because we've never had trouble finding a place to stay.

The coordinates below are all the spots we stayed during our time in Alaska except for a few random roadside pull-offs not worth mentioning. If you're unfamiliar with using coordinates, simply copy them into your map and the navigation will direct you there or as close as the established road will take you and then just use your good sense.

Also note, these locations were gathered during the summer of 2021. As time rolls on, free camping sites tend to change or get closed. That's why apps like iOverlander are so great because if you visit a spot and there is a new no camping sign, you can update the listing for other travelers.

The problem with sites like iOverlander and even in sharing these coordinates with you here is that places tend to get overrun. Van life has exploded in the last few years meaning there are tons of folks on the road and still only a few spots listed online. If there's only one campsite in a town, that campsite is going to get busy. If travelers aren't considerate to the community or leave trash and ruin a space, all this free camping can get shut down in an instant. There's also already a perception of vanlifers that we are not the kind of folks you want in your town. There are many cities and towns implementing bans on sleeping in vehicles. The more we push the boundaries on our behavior, the more likely we will get kicked out for good. Getting a spot closed isn't the only negative that can come from ruining it. There's also the sadness and the negative ramifications of environmental degradation.

We offer you these locations, in order of our travels, in good faith and trust that our FnA Family are going to do right by these beautiful places. Please do not share these places on community apps unless they are already listed and you want to leave a review or an update.

Now go forth and boondock, leave no trace, and have an absolute blast.

- **Anchorage** (61.20082, -149.95195) Residential street outside a park in a busy neighborhood. Listed as Residential Neighborhood on iOverlander.
- **Seaward Highway** (61.0060816, -149.6888015) Near Beluga Point, watch the world-famous bore tide roll in and the surfers ride out then wait for the waters to swell and the belugas to swim by.
- **Girdwood (downtown)** (60.962544, -149.136423) 72-hour stay permitted in any of the parking spaces surrounding the center of town.
- **Girdwood (trailhead)** (60.995504, -149.092745) Not technically allowed but there were multiple campers there both times we went.
- **Girdwood (private lake, potentially closed)** (60.7859896, -148.8569204) This spot was lovely, you could back right up on the lake. Some friends visited here after the fact, and it was closed. Worth a look and there are other spots nearby.
- **Whittier** (60.790230, -148.613050) End of the road with amazing views.
- **Seward** (60.166800, -149.498570) A set of large rocks mark the entrance to the riverbed. Drive slowly on your way in as it's one lane and then take your pick of spots when you get out to the riverbed. The further away from the entrance the better and there's little to no worry of the river rising so high you get stuck.

- **Cooper Landing (super-secret lakeside)**
(Download the coordinates)
https://fnavanlife.com/best-kept-secret-in-alaska/ Because this spot is so precious and a local gem, we're going to ask you to take one more step to get it. Sign up here and we will send you the coordinates directly to your inbox.

- **Watson Lake** (60.535970, -150.461319) This free campground has a pit toilet and a boat launch. When we were there, we got swarmed by mosquitos.

- **Soldotna** (60.44799, -151.28203) Camp at Fred Meyers or drive 20 minutes west to this beach overlook.

- **Homer (campground)** (59.607839, -151.436711) Fishing Hole Campground $20 a night.

- **Homer (stealth park)** (59.603662, -151.426419) Stealth required for this spot. Great for a few nights but pretend you're not home.

- **Eklutna Lake (upper)** (61.423147, -149.202312) There are many good-sized pull offs along the road to Eklutna, this is the one we decided on. There was a fair bit of trash, and we did our part to fill a bag before we left.

- **Eklutna Lake (lower)** (61.448923, -149.372236) Across the street from the Thunderbird Falls parking lot where there are pit toilets.

- **Palmer (in town)** (61.60858, -149.06924) Good spot for the night right in town, a local guy lived there full-time when we were in town.

- **Palmer (riverside)** (61.73302, -148.75185) Many spots by the river so have your pick.
- **Hatcher Pass** (61.77326, -149.32989) You can go much deeper from here but we decided to be less adventurous and stay right at the entrance with a great view of the pass.
- **Glacier View** (61.79558, -147.79796) Not a huge spot but we had three vans down here no problem. Rafting trips depart from here so don't block river access.
- **Glennallen** (62.08141, -145.43414) Cliffside camp spot with amazing views.
- **Valdez (lakeside)** (61.08445, -146.17441) Great spot right on the water, just make sure you don't block access to folks wanting to drop their various watercrafts into the water.
- **Valdez (peninsula)** (61.07719, -146.17925) We stayed here one night but it felt much more exposed than our other location in town, but the view was crazy, and the topography is very cool.
- **Denali Highway** (63.09783, -147.49635) There are endless places to stay along this highway so have your pick. This is where we wanted to stay but ended up just past this spot, over the bridge, at the first pull-off to the right.
- **Talkeetna** (62.32318, -150.11265) Park right downtown around a park that has pit toilets.

- **Fairbanks (pull off)** (64.784746, -148.239603) On route to Fairbanks from Denali a very big pull-off which is perfect if you want to stay out of the city noise and lights.
- **Fairbanks (hostel)** (64.827190, -147.807245) Talk to the front desk to see about parking here. They might charge or you might be able to sweet talk your way into a night or two.
- **Chena Hot Springs** (64.94502, -146.25188) You can pay to camp at Chena or just down the road there are lots of pull offs including this one.
- **Dalton Highway** (65.27791, -148.13228) There are many places to camp along this highway. We stayed here for one night on our way North.
- **Arctic Circle** (66.557667, -150.792687) Brand new BLM campground.

# Accompanying YouTube Video Series

If you are not familiar with FnA Van Life, allow me to introduce ourselves. FnA stands for Frankie and Alex – you know, the folks behind this book. We've been sharing our adventures on the road via YouTube since late 2019 when we were finishing up our first van build and getting ready to hit the road. Since then, we've been incredibly fortunate to have grown an audience that cheers us on and supports us through good times and bad. We are incredibly grateful for the slice of success we've achieved on YouTube because it enables us to continue traveling and creating guides like this.

Making YouTube videos for us is a diary of our adventures. Many of the stories in this book were imprinted into my memories while editing our escapades. Memories are funny like that. Most moments in our lives gently fade away without much passing thought. But when you relive those moments, like by rewatching a video or writing about it in a journal, those impressions deepen and stay with you longer.

Of course, some moments never leave you because they have such a strong emotional impact including the day-to-day stuff: a meal shared with a loved one; the random walk you took on the beach; the way you felt behind the camera when you were sad or angry but trying hard not to show it.

At this point most of my memories are a strange mix of reality and video production. Do I remember the four-wheeling exclusion with Kevin like it happened on that day, or like it happened in the video? It's impossible to know but I am glad to have these video logs (vlogs) of our time here in Alaska and everywhere else. One day if all my memories fade away and I'm sitting under a heavy quilt somewhere cozy, I'll be able to watch these videos and remember what a freaking blast our first visit to Alaska was.

Watch the entire series here: https://fnavanlife.com/alaska-guide

# Where to Next?

Our adventures aren't finished yet. There is still so much of America, Canada, Mexico, and Central America we want to explore (well really the whole world but that's where we can drive… for now). We would love for you to join us for these adventures as we share all the ups, downs, ins, and outs of living on the road full time.

- Follow our YouTube adventures here:

    **https://www.youtube.com/fnavanlife**

- Check out of Instagram (our DMs are always open):

    **https://www.instagram.com/fnavanlife**

- Get exclusive behind the scenes content and help us continue to travel here:

    **https://www.fnavanlife.com/patreon**

- For your new favorite podcast, listen here:

    **https://www.anchor.fm/fnavanlife**

Wherever you end up, we would love to hear if this guide was helpful in planning your Alaskan adventure. If you enjoyed this read, please leave a review on Amazon.

A huge thank you to all the friends who made our time in Alaska amazing and who shared their experiences with us to include in this guide. Find our friends on Instagram here and see what their Alaska adventures looked like for yourself. Tell them FnA sent you:

- Adaptive Humanity

    https://www.instagram.com/adaptivehumanity/

- Drifter Journey

    https://www.instagram.com/drifter.journey/

- Fennimore's Adventure More

    https://www.instagram.com/fenimoresadventuremore/

- Out of This Van

    https://www.instagram.com/outofthisvan/

- Newstate Nomads

    https://www.instagram.com/newstatenomads/

- Travels with Kevan

    https://www.instagram.com/travelswithkevan/

My last thank you goes out to Frankie, although he didn't help write this guide, he drove every single mile of our adventure. I will gladly be his copilot for life and can't wait to see where the winding road of life takes us. It can't be bumpier than the Dalton.

May all your travels be Fn'A,
    Xo Alex

Made in the USA
Columbia, SC
14 January 2022